UNDERSTANDING KUBERNETES FOR CONTAINER ORCHESTRATION

Managing containerized
applications using Kubernetes for
scaling and automating
deployments

NATHAN WESTWOOD

TABLE OF CONTENTS

ABOUT THE AUTHOR!

Dr. Nathan Westwood

Biography:

Dr. Nathan Westwood is a pioneering technologist known for his exceptional contributions to the fields of software development, cloud computing, and artificial intelligence. With a passion for innovation and a relentless drive to solve complex problems, Nathan has become a prominent figure in the tech industry, shaping the future of digital technology.

Born and raised in Silicon Valley, Nathan's interest in technology started at a young age. His fascination with computers and coding led him to pursue a degree in Computer Science from Stanford University, where he excelled academically and honed his skills in programming and software engineering. During his time at Stanford, Nathan was involved in several cutting-edge projects that sparked his interest in AI and cloud technologies.

After graduating, Nathan joined a leading tech firm where he played a key role in developing cloud-based solutions that revolutionized data storage and analytics. His work in the early stages of cloud computing set the foundation for modern infrastructure-as-a-service (IaaS) platforms, earning him recognition as one of the industry's emerging stars. As a lead engineer, Nathan was instrumental in launching products that have since become industry standards.

Nathan's entrepreneurial spirit led him to co-found his own tech startup focused on AI-driven automation tools for businesses. Under his leadership, the company rapidly gained traction, attracting both investors and clients who were eager to leverage his innovative AI solutions to streamline operations and improve efficiency. Nathan's commitment to pushing the boundaries of what's possible in tech quickly earned him a reputation as a visionary leader.

Known for his expertise in machine learning, Nathan has also worked with several large tech companies, advising on the integration of AI and data science into their operations. His work has spanned various sectors, including healthcare, finance, and manufacturing, where he has helped organizations harness the power of data and automation to achieve exponential growth.

Beyond his technical achievements, Nathan is a sought-after speaker at global tech conferences, where he shares his insights on the future of cloud computing, artificial intelligence, and the ethical challenges posed by emerging technologies. His thought leadership and commitment to ethical innovation have made him a respected voice in the tech community.

In addition to his professional accomplishments, Nathan is deeply passionate about mentoring the next generation of tech leaders. He regularly contributes to educational programs and initiatives designed to inspire young minds and equip them with the skills necessary to thrive in the ever-evolving tech landscape.

Nathan Westwood continues to be a trailblazer in the tech industry, shaping the future of technology with his innovative ideas, entrepreneurial spirit, and commitment to making a positive impact on the world.

CHAPTER 1: INTRODUCTION TO KUBERNETES AND CONTAINERIZATION

Welcome to the world of containerization and Kubernetes! This chapter is your gateway to understanding how modern applications are built, deployed, and managed. We'll explore the idea of containerization, explain why Kubernetes has become the go-to tool for managing containers, and take a brief look at how this technology evolved over time. Finally, we'll set the stage for practical work, so you can roll up your sleeves and try your hand at some hands-on projects.

Throughout this chapter, we'll keep things straightforward, breaking down complex ideas into manageable pieces. We'll use everyday examples, analogies, and step-by-step instructions so that even if you're just getting started, you can follow along. Let's begin!

Section 1: What is Containerization?

Imagine you're packing for a trip. You have a suitcase where you place your clothes, shoes, and accessories. Each item is neatly folded, packed, and separated so that nothing gets lost or mixed up. Now, think about if you had a system where every suitcase could be moved from place to place without worrying about what's inside—

your items remain exactly as you packed them, regardless of where you travel.

That's containerization in a nutshell. Instead of packing clothes, you're packing an entire application along with all its dependencies—libraries, binaries, and configuration files. This "container" can be moved from one environment to another without changes, ensuring that the application runs exactly the same everywhere.

Key Features of Containerization

- **Isolation:** Each container runs in its own separate environment, much like each suitcase keeps your belongings separate. This isolation means that the application won't interfere with others running on the same system.

- **Portability:** Just like a suitcase can be taken on a plane, a container can be easily moved between different computing environments. Whether it's your laptop, a server in a data center, or a cloud platform, containers work the same way.

- **Consistency:** When you build a container, you include everything the application needs. That way, if you run the container anywhere, it behaves exactly as expected. This consistency eliminates the "it works on my machine" problem that many developers face.

- **Efficiency:** Containers share the same operating system kernel, which means they use fewer resources than traditional virtual machines. This allows you to run more containers on a single server, making your infrastructure more efficient.

Real-World Analogy: The Food Delivery Box

Consider a food delivery service. When you order your favorite dish, the restaurant packages it into a container (a box) that keeps it fresh and prevents it from spilling or mixing with other items. Whether the box is transported across town or across the country, the food inside stays just the way it was when it left the kitchen. This is very similar to how a container works in computing.

Hands-On Project: Build Your First Container

Let's start with a simple project to see containerization in action.

Project: Containerizing a "Hello, World!" Application

Objective:
Learn how to create a container for a simple application that prints "Hello, World!" to the screen.

Requirements:

- A computer with Docker installed. If you haven't installed Docker yet, check out the official Docker website for installation guides for your operating system.

- A text editor to create and edit files.

Steps:

1. **Create a Project Directory:**
   Open your terminal or command prompt and create a new directory for your project.

bash

```
mkdir hello-container
cd hello-container
```

2. **Write a Simple Application:**
   Create a file named app.py with the following content:

python

```
print("Hello, World!")
```
This script simply prints a greeting to the console.

3. **Create a Dockerfile:**
   A Dockerfile is a set of instructions that Docker uses to build a container image. Create a file named Dockerfile (with no file extension) in the same directory, and add the following lines:

dockerfile

```
# Use an official Python runtime as the base image
FROM python:3.9-slim

# Set the working directory in the container
WORKDIR /app


# Copy the current directory contents into the container at /app
COPY . /app

# Run the command to execute the application
CMD ["python", "app.py"]
```
This Dockerfile tells Docker to use a lightweight version of Python, copy your code into the container, and run your application.

4. **Build the Container Image:**
   In your terminal, run the following command:

bash

```
docker build -t hello-container .
```
This command builds a container image with the tag hello-container.

5. **Run the Container:**

   Once the build completes, run your container:

bash

docker run hello-container
You should see "Hello, World!" printed in your terminal.

6. **Troubleshooting Tips:**

   o   If the build fails, check your Dockerfile for typos.

   o   Ensure Docker is running on your system.

   o   If you see errors when running the container, verify that the file paths in the Dockerfile are correct.

This simple project introduces the key concepts behind containerization and shows how you can package an application with all its dependencies. As you work through the project, consider how this same approach can be applied to more complex applications.

Section 2: Why Kubernetes?

Now that we understand what containerization is and have seen a simple example in action, you might be wondering: why do we need something like Kubernetes? After all, Docker already lets you run containers on your machine. Kubernetes steps in to solve a more complex challenge: managing many containers across multiple machines.

The Need for Container Orchestration

Imagine you run a busy restaurant with dozens of chefs, waiters, and a bustling kitchen. Now, picture trying to coordinate every single activity without a system in place. Chaos would quickly ensue, orders might be forgotten, and efficiency would suffer.

Similarly, when you deploy an application in containers, you might have dozens, hundreds, or even thousands of containers running on different machines. Manually managing these containers would be overwhelming. This is where container orchestration comes in. It automates the deployment, scaling, and management of containerized applications.

How Kubernetes Helps

Kubernetes is like the restaurant manager who ensures that every chef and waiter knows their role, that orders are efficiently processed, and that the kitchen runs smoothly even during peak hours. It provides a framework for automating the deployment, scaling, and operations of application containers across clusters of hosts.

Here are some key reasons why Kubernetes is so popular:

- **Automated Scaling:**
  Kubernetes can automatically adjust the number of running containers based on traffic and resource utilization. This means your application can handle a sudden influx of users without manual intervention.

- **Self-Healing:**
  If a container fails, Kubernetes will restart or replace it. This self-healing capability ensures that your application remains available and resilient.

- **Load Balancing:**
  Kubernetes distributes network traffic to ensure that no

single container is overwhelmed. This load balancing ensures smooth and reliable performance.

- **Efficient Resource Utilization:**
  By efficiently managing container placement, Kubernetes helps you make the best use of your infrastructure, reducing waste and lowering costs.

- **Declarative Configuration:**
  You describe the desired state of your application, and Kubernetes works to maintain that state. This approach simplifies management and reduces errors.

Real-World Analogy: The City Traffic Control Center

Imagine a busy city where traffic lights are synchronized to keep vehicles moving smoothly. The traffic control center constantly monitors the flow of vehicles and adjusts the lights to prevent jams. Kubernetes works in a similar way for containers. It monitors your applications, makes adjustments to ensure everything runs smoothly, and intervenes automatically when something goes wrong.

Hands-On Project: Deploying a Multi-Container Application

Let's put these ideas into practice with a hands-on project that involves deploying a simple multi-container application using Kubernetes.

Project: Deploying a Basic Web Application on Kubernetes

Objective:
Deploy a web application that consists of a frontend and a backend service, and see how Kubernetes manages the containers.

Requirements:

- A computer with Docker and Minikube (or another local Kubernetes solution) installed.

- A text editor for creating configuration files.

Steps:

1. **Set Up a Local Kubernetes Cluster:**
   Start by launching your local Kubernetes cluster using Minikube. Open your terminal and run:

bash

```
minikube start
```

This command sets up a local cluster that will mimic a real-world Kubernetes environment.

2. **Create Deployment Manifests:**
   In Kubernetes, a deployment defines how an application is run. Create a directory called k8s-deployments and navigate into it:

bash

```
mkdir k8s-deployments
cd k8s-deployments
```

Create a file called frontend-deployment.yaml with the following content:
yaml

```
apiVersion: apps/v1
kind: Deployment
```

```yaml
metadata:
  name: frontend-deployment
spec:
  replicas: 2
  selector:
    matchLabels:
      app: frontend
  template:
    metadata:
      labels:
        app: frontend
    spec:
      containers:
      - name: frontend
        image: nginx:alpine
        ports:
        - containerPort: 80
```

This file tells Kubernetes to run two instances (replicas) of a simple Nginx container that will serve as the frontend.

Next, create a file called backend-deployment.yaml:

yaml

```yaml
apiVersion: apps/v1
kind: Deployment
metadata:
  name: backend-deployment
spec:
  replicas: 2
  selector:
    matchLabels:
      app: backend
  template:
    metadata:
      labels:
        app: backend
    spec:
      containers:
      - name: backend
        image: hashicorp/http-echo
        args:
```

```
- "-text=Hello from the backend"
ports:
- containerPort: 5678
```

This deployment creates two replicas of a container that responds with a simple text message.

3. **Create Service Manifests:**
   To allow these deployments to be accessed, you need to create services. Create a file named frontend-service.yaml:

```yaml
apiVersion: v1
kind: Service
metadata:
  name: frontend-service
spec:
  selector:
    app: frontend
  ports:
  - protocol: TCP
    port: 80
    targetPort: 80
  type: NodePort
```

And for the backend, create backend-service.yaml:

```yaml
apiVersion: v1
kind: Service
metadata:
  name: backend-service
spec:
  selector:
    app: backend
  ports:
  - protocol: TCP
    port: 80
    targetPort: 5678
  type: ClusterIP
```

The frontend service is accessible externally via a NodePort, while the backend is only accessible within the cluster.

4. Deploy to Kubernetes:

Apply the deployments and services using kubectl:

bash

```
kubectl apply -f frontend-deployment.yaml
kubectl apply -f backend-deployment.yaml
kubectl apply -f frontend-service.yaml
kubectl apply -f backend-service.yaml
```

You can check the status of your deployments by running:

bash

```
kubectl get deployments
kubectl get pods
```

If everything is running correctly, you should see all pods in a "Running" state.

Access the Frontend:
To view the frontend, get the URL for your Minikube cluster:

bash

```
minikube service frontend-service --url
```

Open the URL in your browser, and you should see the default Nginx page.

Testing the Backend:
Since the backend service is only accessible within the cluster, you can test it by running:

bash

```
kubectl run curlpod --image=radial/busyboxplus:curl -i --tty
```

Then, within the busybox pod, run:

bash

```
curl backend-service
```

You should see the message "Hello from the backend."

This project gives you a taste of how Kubernetes manages containerized applications, automatically handling aspects like replication and service discovery.

Section 3: Brief History and Evolution

Before we dive deeper into the mechanics of Kubernetes, it's useful to understand how we arrived here. The history of containerization and Kubernetes is a story of evolving needs in software development and deployment.

Early Days: Virtual Machines and Their Limitations

For many years, virtual machines (VMs) were the standard method for isolating and running applications on a shared infrastructure. VMs allowed multiple operating systems to run on a single physical server by abstracting hardware resources. However, VMs have their downsides:

- **Resource Heavy:**
  Each VM includes not just the application but an entire operating system, leading to significant overhead.

- **Slow Boot Times:**
  Starting up a VM can take minutes, which is problematic for applications that require rapid scaling.

- **Inefficient Resource Utilization:**
  Running multiple VMs on a single server often leads to wasted resources, as each VM requires its own dedicated resources.

The Emergence of Containers

The idea behind containers was to create a lightweight, efficient alternative to VMs. Containers share the host operating system's kernel, which drastically reduces overhead and allows for faster startup times. This concept isn't entirely new; technologies like chroot and LXC (Linux Containers) paved the way. However, containers as we know them today gained momentum with the introduction of Docker around 2013. Docker popularized the concept by making containerization accessible to developers and operations teams alike.

The Birth of Kubernetes

While Docker provided an excellent way to package applications, it didn't address the challenge of managing hundreds or thousands of containers. As applications grew in complexity and scale, the need for an orchestration tool became clear.

Kubernetes was originally developed by Google, drawing on their extensive experience running containers in production. In 2014, Google released Kubernetes as an open-source project, which quickly gained traction within the developer community. Kubernetes offered a powerful, flexible system to deploy, scale, and manage containerized applications, solving many of the issues encountered with traditional VM setups and even with early container management tools.

Key Milestones in Kubernetes Evolution

- **2014:**
  Kubernetes is released as an open-source project, capturing the attention of developers worldwide.

- **2015:**
  Major cloud providers begin integrating Kubernetes into their platforms, making it accessible to a broader audience.

- **2016-2017:**
  Kubernetes matures rapidly, with regular updates, enhanced security features, and broader community support.

- **Today:**
  Kubernetes is the leading container orchestration platform used by enterprises, startups, and hobbyists alike.

This evolution highlights the shift in the software industry toward microservices architectures, where applications are broken down into smaller, independently deployable services. Kubernetes is at the forefront of this shift, providing the tools needed to manage these distributed systems efficiently.

Hands-On Project: Exploring Kubernetes History with a Timeline Visualization

While the history of Kubernetes might seem like a series of dates and events, visualizing this timeline can help bring the evolution to life.

Project: Creating a Timeline of Kubernetes Milestones

Objective:
Create a simple timeline that highlights key milestones in the evolution of Kubernetes.

Requirements:

- A computer with Python installed.

- A text editor to create a Python script.

- Basic familiarity with Python libraries such as Matplotlib.

Steps:

1. **Set Up Your Python Environment:**
   Ensure you have Python installed. You can use a virtual environment if you prefer.

bash

```
python -m venv timeline-env
source timeline-env/bin/activate   # On Windows use `timeline-env\Scripts\activate`
pip install matplotlib
```

2. **Create a Python Script:**
   Create a file named k8s_timeline.py and add the following code:

python

```python
import matplotlib.pyplot as plt

# Milestones and their years
milestones = {
    "Docker popularizes containers": 2013,
    "Kubernetes open-sourced": 2014,
    "Cloud providers integrate Kubernetes": 2015,
    "Kubernetes matures with regular updates": 2016,
    "Kubernetes becomes industry standard": 2020
}

events = list(milestones.keys())
years = list(milestones.values())

plt.figure(figsize=(10, 4))
plt.hlines(1, min(years) - 1, max(years) + 1, colors='gray', linestyles='dashed')
plt.scatter(years, [1] * len(years), s=100, color='blue')

for event, year in milestones.items():
    plt.text(year, 1.05, f"{year}\n{event}", horizontalalignment='center')

plt.yticks([])
```

```
plt.xlabel("Year")
plt.title("Key Milestones in the Evolution of Kubernetes")
plt.tight_layout()
plt.show()
```

3. **Run the Script:**

   Execute the script by running:

bash

```
python k8s_timeline.py
```

A window should appear displaying the timeline with key milestones. This visualization not only makes the history more tangible but also reinforces the rapid pace of development in container orchestration.

This project demonstrates that even historical data can be explored through practical applications, reinforcing how Kubernetes has become a pivotal technology.

Section 4: Setting the Stage for Practical Work

With an understanding of what containerization is and why Kubernetes matters, it's time to prepare for hands-on work. The projects and examples provided in this chapter are just the beginning. As you progress, you'll work on increasingly complex tasks, from scaling applications to integrating continuous deployment pipelines.

Preparing Your Environment

Before diving into more advanced projects, you need a suitable setup. Here are the basic components you'll need:

- **Local Development Environment:**
  Tools like Docker and Minikube (or Kind) let you run containers and a local Kubernetes cluster on your own computer.

- **Code Editor:**
  A good code editor can make all the difference. Options like Visual Studio Code or Sublime Text are popular choices among developers for their ease of use and helpful features.

- **Command-Line Interface:**
  Familiarity with the terminal will come in handy. Many tasks in containerization and Kubernetes involve command-line commands, so take your time to get comfortable with basic commands like navigating directories, running scripts, and managing processes.

Tips for Beginners

Starting out can feel overwhelming, but remember that every small step builds your knowledge and confidence. Here are some pointers to help you along the way:

- **Take It One Step at a Time:**
  Don't try to absorb everything at once. Break down each project into manageable tasks and focus on one aspect before moving on to the next.

- **Experiment and Learn from Mistakes:**
  It's perfectly normal to encounter errors. Use them as learning opportunities. If something doesn't work as expected, take a moment to troubleshoot and understand what went wrong.

- **Use the Community:**
  The Kubernetes community is active and supportive. Forums, chat groups, and online tutorials can be excellent resources when you need help or want to learn new techniques.

Real-World Applications and Challenges

Kubernetes is used in many industries to manage containerized applications. Let's look at a few examples:

- **Manufacturing:**
  In manufacturing, applications need to process data from sensors in real-time, manage complex workflows, and ensure minimal downtime. Kubernetes can help by automatically scaling applications and recovering quickly from failures.

- **Healthcare:**
  In healthcare, reliability and security are paramount. Kubernetes supports secure deployments and can manage sensitive data with minimal risk, ensuring that healthcare applications remain available and compliant with regulations.

- **Logistics:**
  Logistics applications often deal with fluctuating workloads, especially during peak shipping seasons. Kubernetes helps by dynamically scaling resources based on demand, ensuring that operations remain smooth even during high-traffic periods.

Hands-On Project: Setting Up Your First Kubernetes Workspace

Now, let's prepare your workspace for further exploration of Kubernetes. This project guides you through installing and configuring the necessary tools.

Project: Installing and Configuring Your Kubernetes Environment

Objective:
Set up a local environment that allows you to experiment with Kubernetes and containerized applications.

Requirements:

- A computer with virtualization support.

- Internet access to download Docker and Minikube.

- Basic command-line skills.

Steps:

1. **Install Docker:**
   Visit the official Docker website and download the installer for your operating system. Follow the installation prompts to get Docker up and running.

   - Verify your installation by opening your terminal and running:

bash

docker --version

You should see a version number indicating that Docker is installed.

2. **Install Minikube:**
    Minikube makes it simple to run a single-node Kubernetes cluster on your local machine.

    o   Download and install Minikube from its official website.

    o   Start Minikube by running:

```bash
minikube start
```

This command creates a local cluster that mimics a real Kubernetes environment.

3. **Install kubectl:**
    Kubectl is the command-line tool for interacting with your Kubernetes cluster.

    o   Download kubectl from the official Kubernetes website.

    o   Verify the installation:

```bash
kubectl version --client
```

You should see version details that confirm kubectl is ready to use.

4. **Test Your Setup:**
    Run a simple command to check the status of your cluster:

```bash
kubectl get nodes
```

You should see a list that includes your local Minikube node.

5. **Document Your Environment:**
    Keep a record of the versions of Docker, Minikube, and

kubectl you're using. This documentation can be helpful for troubleshooting and future upgrades.

By completing this project, you'll have a fully functional workspace to experiment with Kubernetes. With this environment, you can start deploying applications, experimenting with configurations, and learning how to manage containerized systems.

Wrapping Up

In this chapter, we've explored the basics of containerization and the role Kubernetes plays in managing modern applications. We started with the idea of containers, using everyday analogies to illustrate how they work and why they're so effective at ensuring consistency and portability. Next, we looked at why Kubernetes is needed to orchestrate these containers, comparing it to managing a busy city's traffic or a well-run restaurant. We also took a brief look at the history and evolution of Kubernetes, providing context for why it has become such a vital tool in today's software development landscape.

We wrapped up with practical, hands-on projects—from containerizing a simple "Hello, World!" application to deploying a basic multi-container web application on Kubernetes, and even creating a timeline visualization of Kubernetes milestones. Each project was designed to be beginner-friendly, with clear, actionable steps and real-world examples that tie back to industries like manufacturing, healthcare, and logistics.

As you move forward, keep in mind that mastering Kubernetes and containerization is a gradual process. Every project you undertake builds your skill set and deepens your understanding of these technologies. Remember, even if things feel challenging at first, persistence and hands-on experimentation are your best tools for success.

In the upcoming chapters, we'll build on this foundation. We'll dive deeper into the inner workings of Kubernetes, explore advanced deployment strategies, and tackle challenges such as scaling, monitoring, and securing containerized applications. Whether you're a beginner eager to learn, a professional looking to expand your toolkit, or a hobbyist interested in exploring new technologies, this book is designed to give you the skills and confidence you need to succeed.

Take a moment to celebrate what you've learned so far. You now understand the core principles of containerization, why Kubernetes has become essential, and the historical context that has shaped today's technological landscape. With your development environment set up and a few projects under your belt, you're ready to take on more complex challenges.

configuration you tweak brings you closer to mastering Kubernetes.

Happy coding, and here's to the exciting path ahead!

CHAPTER 2: GETTING STARTED WITH KUBERNETES

Welcome to the start of your hands-on experience with Kubernetes! In this chapter, we will guide you through the process of setting up your own local environment so that you can experiment, learn, and build confidence with container orchestration. We will break down the key building blocks of Kubernetes such as Pods, Nodes, Clusters, and Services. Along the way, you'll create your very first Pod and run a simple application on your local cluster. Whether you're a hobbyist, a beginner, or someone looking to refine your skills, this chapter will provide you with clear, practical instructions to move forward.

1. Installing and Configuring a Local Environment

Before you can run any applications with Kubernetes, you need to create an environment where you can test your deployments. A local environment is a great starting point. Not only does it let you try out commands and configurations without affecting production systems, but it also gives you a playground to experiment freely.

1.1. Why a Local Environment?

Imagine you are learning to cook with a new recipe. Before serving it at a big event, you would first practice in your own kitchen. A local Kubernetes setup works similarly. It allows you to explore, learn from mistakes, and become comfortable with the commands and processes before scaling up to larger environments. By working locally, you have complete control over the environment and can easily reset or adjust configurations as needed.

1.2. Essential Tools

To get started, there are three primary tools you will need:

- **Docker:** This software packages your applications into containers.

- **Minikube:** A tool that runs a single-node Kubernetes cluster on your local machine.

- **kubectl:** The command-line interface that lets you interact with your Kubernetes cluster.

These tools are available on multiple operating systems. Check out the official websites for Docker, Minikube, and Kubernetes to find installation instructions specific to your system. For now, let's assume you have a computer running Windows, macOS, or a popular Linux distribution.

1.3. Step-by-Step Installation

Let's break down the installation process into clear steps.

Step 1: Installing Docker

1. **Download Docker:**
   Head over to the Docker website and download the installer for your operating system. Follow the prompts to install Docker on your computer.

2. **Verify Installation:**
   Open your terminal (or command prompt) and type:

```bash
docker --version
```

This command should return a version number, confirming that Docker is ready to use.

3. **Troubleshooting Tip:**
   If you encounter issues, check that your system meets the minimum requirements and that virtualization is enabled in your BIOS settings.

Step 2: Installing Minikube

1. **Download Minikube:**
   Visit the Minikube GitHub releases page or the official documentation. Download the version appropriate for your system.

2. **Install Minikube:**
   On Windows, you might use an installer; on macOS, Homebrew is a popular choice; on Linux, you can use a package manager or download the binary directly.

3. **Start Minikube:**
   Once installed, open your terminal and start the local Kubernetes cluster with:

```bash
minikube start
```

This command sets up a single-node cluster on your computer.

4. **Verify Cluster Status:**
   Check the status by running:

```bash
minikube status
```

You should see that all components (the cluster, kubelet, etc.) are running properly.

Step 3: Installing kubectl

1. **Download kubectl:**
   The official Kubernetes website provides instructions for installing kubectl on all major platforms.

2. **Install and Configure:**
   Follow the installation instructions carefully. Once installed, verify it with:

```bash
kubectl version --client
```

This command returns version details that confirm kubectl is set up.

3. **Set Up Environment Variables:**
   In some cases, you might need to add the kubectl executable to your system's PATH variable for easy access from the terminal.

1.4. Putting It All Together

After installing Docker, Minikube, and kubectl, you have a local environment ready for exploration. This setup is like a test kitchen where you can try out recipes without any fear of ruining your main dish. Each tool plays an essential role:

- Docker handles containerization.

- Minikube simulates a Kubernetes cluster.

- kubectl allows you to manage the cluster.

Spend a few minutes getting comfortable with the basic commands for each tool. Run simple commands to check their status and familiarize yourself with their outputs. A little practice now will pay off when you start creating more complex deployments.

---

2. Overview of Key Components

Now that your local environment is set up, let's break down the key components that make Kubernetes tick. Understanding these building blocks will help you see how everything fits together and give you the confidence to start managing your own deployments.

2.1. Pods

A Pod is the smallest and simplest unit in the Kubernetes model. Think of a Pod as a small container that holds one or more application containers. These containers share the same network namespace and storage volumes, which means they can easily communicate with each other.

Real-World Analogy: The Delivery Box

Consider a delivery box that holds several items. The items are packaged together so that when the box is moved, everything inside remains together. Similarly, containers in a Pod are managed as a single unit, making deployment and scaling easier.

Why Use Pods?

- **Grouping:**
  When you need multiple containers to work together, Pods allow them to be scheduled on the same node.

- **Communication:**
  Containers in a Pod can share data and communicate via localhost.

- **Scaling:**
  Pods can be replicated to handle increased load.

2.2. Nodes

Nodes are the worker machines in a Kubernetes cluster. They can be physical or virtual machines that run the containerized applications. Each node is managed by the Kubernetes control plane and includes services to run the containers, report on the node's health, and provide networking capabilities.

Real-World Analogy: The Factory Floor

Imagine a factory with several production lines. Each production line (node) has the tools and resources necessary to complete specific tasks. Similarly, nodes provide the infrastructure needed to run your Pods.

Key Points About Nodes

- **Resources:**
  Each node has CPU, memory, and storage that are allocated to running containers.

- **Communication:**
  Nodes are connected in a network, enabling Pods on different nodes to communicate seamlessly.

- **Management:**
  The control plane monitors nodes and takes action if one fails.

2.3. Clusters

A Kubernetes cluster is a group of nodes managed as a single entity. The cluster includes a control plane, which orchestrates how and where Pods run, and the worker nodes that run the actual applications.

Real-World Analogy: The Entire Restaurant

Think of a cluster as a full-service restaurant. The control plane is like the management team that assigns tasks, monitors service, and ensures everything is running smoothly, while the nodes are the individual stations in the restaurant where the work gets done.

Benefits of Clusters

- **Scalability:**
  Clusters allow you to scale applications across multiple machines.

- **Resilience:**
  If one node fails, the control plane redistributes Pods to other available nodes.

- **Centralized Management:**
  The cluster provides a unified interface for deploying and managing applications.

2.4. Services

Services in Kubernetes expose your Pods to the outside world or to other Pods within the cluster. A Service defines a logical set of Pods and a policy to access them. Services ensure that applications remain reachable even if Pods are added or removed.

Real-World Analogy: The Customer Service Desk

Imagine a customer service desk at a busy shopping center. No matter how many stores (Pods) change locations or numbers, customers know where to go to get help. Services act like that central desk, routing traffic to the correct Pods.

Types of Services

- **ClusterIP:**
  Exposes the service on an internal IP in the cluster. This is the default type.

- **NodePort:**
  Exposes the service on the IP of each node at a static port.

- **LoadBalancer:**
  Uses an external load balancer to route traffic to the service.

2.5. Bringing the Components Together

Imagine you're setting up a small business with different departments (Pods) operating on various floors (Nodes) within a building (Cluster). To ensure customers can reach the right department, you have a reception desk (Service) that directs traffic accordingly. This analogy shows how the key components of Kubernetes work together to manage and scale your applications.

Spend some time reviewing these components and considering how they might apply to your own projects. Once you're comfortable with these ideas, you'll be ready to take the next step—creating your very first Pod.

3. First Steps: Creating Your First Pod

One of the most exciting moments in learning Kubernetes is creating and running your very first Pod. This exercise not only builds confidence but also demonstrates the power of Kubernetes in a tangible way. We'll walk through the process step by step.

3.1. Understanding the Pod Definition

To create a Pod, you write a configuration file, usually in YAML format, that describes the desired state of the Pod. This file specifies which container image to use, any ports that need to be opened, and other relevant configurations.

Breaking Down a Pod Configuration

Let's consider a simple Pod configuration:

- **apiVersion:**
  Indicates which version of the Kubernetes API to use.

- **kind:**
  Tells Kubernetes that this configuration is for a Pod.

- **metadata:**
  Provides data about the Pod, such as its name and labels.

- **spec:**
  Defines the details of the Pod, including the container image and any settings for that container.

3.2. Writing Your First Pod Configuration

Let's write a basic configuration for a Pod that runs a simple application. Open your favorite text editor and create a file named first-pod.yaml with the following content:

yaml

```
apiVersion: v1
kind: Pod
metadata:
  name: my-first-pod
  labels:
    app: demo
spec:
  containers:
  - name: demo-container
    image: busybox
    command: ["sh", "-c", "echo 'Hello from Kubernetes!' && sleep 3600"]
```

Explanation:

- **apiVersion and kind:**
  These lines tell Kubernetes that you are creating a Pod using version 1 of the API.

- **metadata:**
  The Pod is named "my-first-pod" and labeled with app: demo for easy identification.

- **spec:**
  Under spec, we define one container named "demo-container." The container uses the busybox image and runs a command that prints a greeting message before sleeping

for an hour. This simple configuration ensures the Pod stays active long enough for you to inspect it.

3.3. Deploying the Pod

With your configuration file in place, it's time to deploy your Pod to the cluster. Open your terminal, navigate to the directory containing first-pod.yaml, and run:

bash

```
kubectl apply -f first-pod.yaml
```
This command instructs Kubernetes to create the Pod based on your configuration.

Verifying the Deployment

After deploying, check the status of your Pod with:

bash

```
kubectl get pods
```
You should see "my-first-pod" listed with a status indicating that it is running. If you want more details about the Pod, use:

bash

```
kubectl describe pod my-first-pod
```
This command shows detailed information about the Pod's configuration, its current status, and any events that have occurred. Take your time to explore these details; they provide valuable insight into how Kubernetes is managing your Pod.

3.4. Cleaning Up

Once you have inspected the Pod and are satisfied with the results, it's a good idea to remove it to keep your environment tidy. Delete the Pod using:

bash

```
kubectl delete pod my-first-pod
```

This command will remove the Pod from your cluster. Practicing clean-up procedures is part of good operational habits and helps keep your workspace organized.

---

4. Hands-on Project: Running a Simple Application on a Local Cluster

Now that you've seen how to create and manage a Pod, it's time to put your skills to the test with a hands-on project. In this project, you will deploy a simple web application to your local Kubernetes cluster. This project is designed to consolidate your learning and give you a practical example of Kubernetes in action.

4.1. Project Overview

In this project, we will deploy a basic web application that displays a simple message on a web page. The application will be containerized, and Kubernetes will manage its deployment and networking. The steps include:

- Creating a container image for the application.

- Writing deployment and service configuration files.

- Applying these configurations to your local cluster.

- Verifying that the application is accessible through a browser.

4.2. Step 1: Creating a Simple Web Application

Let's start by writing a very simple web application. For this example, we'll use Python with the Flask framework, which is known for its ease of use.

Creating the Application Code

1. **Set Up a New Directory:**
   Create a new directory for the project:

bash

```
mkdir simple-web-app
cd simple-web-app
```

2. **Create the Application File:**
   Create a file called app.py with the following content:

python

```
from flask import Flask

app = Flask(__name__)

@app.route('/')
def home():
    return "Hello from Kubernetes on your local cluster!"

if __name__ == '__main__':
    app.run(host='0.0.0.0', port=5000)
```

This code sets up a basic Flask web application that responds to requests at the root URL.

3. **Create a Requirements File:**
   Create a file named requirements.txt and add:

txt

flask

This file lists the Python packages needed to run your application.

4.3. Step 2: Containerizing the Application

Next, we will create a Dockerfile to containerize the web application.

Writing the Dockerfile

Create a file named Dockerfile in the same directory with the following content:

dockerfile

```
# Use a lightweight Python image as the base
FROM python:3.9-slim

# Set the working directory inside the container
WORKDIR /app


# Copy the current directory contents into the container
COPY . /app

# Install the dependencies from requirements.txt
RUN pip install --no-cache-dir -r requirements.txt

# Expose port 5000 for the Flask application
EXPOSE 5000

# Run the application
CMD ["python", "app.py"]
```

This Dockerfile specifies how to build the container image. It uses a slim version of Python, copies your application code into the container, installs the necessary packages, and then runs the Flask application.

Building the Container Image

With the Dockerfile ready, build your container image using Docker:

bash

```
docker build -t simple-web-app .
```
This command creates a Docker image tagged as simple-web-app. The build process fetches the base image, copies your files, installs Flask, and sets up the application.

Testing the Container Locally

Before moving on to Kubernetes, let's verify that your container works as expected. Run the container locally:

bash

```
docker run -p 5000:5000 simple-web-app
```
Now, open your browser and go to http://localhost:5000. You should see the message: "Hello from Kubernetes on your local cluster!" If everything works fine, stop the container (using Ctrl+C in your terminal) to proceed with the Kubernetes deployment.

4.4. Step 3: Creating Kubernetes Deployment and Service Files

To run your application on Kubernetes, you need two main configuration files:

- A **Deployment** file to manage the creation and scaling of Pods.

- A **Service** file to expose the application externally.

Creating the Deployment Configuration

Create a new file called deployment.yaml with the following content:

yaml

```
apiVersion: apps/v1
kind: Deployment
metadata:
 name: web-app-deployment
 labels:
  app: simple-web-app
spec:
 replicas: 2
 selector:
  matchLabels:
   app: simple-web-app
 template:
  metadata:
   labels:
    app: simple-web-app
  spec:
   containers:
   - name: web-app-container
    image: simple-web-app:latest
    ports:
    - containerPort: 5000
```

Explanation:

- **replicas:**
  We are running two instances of the web application.

- **selector and template:**
  These lines ensure that the Pods are correctly labeled,
  making it easier for the Service to identify them.

- **containerPort:**
  Specifies the port on which the application is running inside
  the container.

Creating the Service Configuration

Now, create a file called service.yaml with the following content:

yaml

```
apiVersion: v1
kind: Service
metadata:
  name: web-app-service
spec:
  type: NodePort
  selector:
    app: simple-web-app
  ports:
  - port: 5000
    targetPort: 5000
    nodePort: 30007
```

Explanation:

- **type: NodePort:**
  This exposes the application on a specific port on your local machine.

- **nodePort:**
  The external port (30007 in this example) through which you can access the application.

4.5. Step 4: Deploying Your Application to Kubernetes

With both configuration files in place, it's time to deploy the application to your local Kubernetes cluster.

1. **Apply the Deployment:**
   In your terminal, navigate to the directory containing deployment.yaml and run:

bash

kubectl apply -f deployment.yaml
This command instructs Kubernetes to create the Pods as specified.

2. **Apply the Service:**
   Next, deploy the service by running:

bash

kubectl apply -f service.yaml
This sets up the networking so you can access your web application.

3. **Verify the Deployment:**
   Check the status of your deployment and Pods:

bash

kubectl get deployments
kubectl get pods
The output should show that your deployment is running and the
Pods are in a healthy state.

4. **Access the Application:**
   Since you specified a NodePort, retrieve the URL by running:

bash

minikube service web-app-service --url
Open the provided URL in your web browser. You should see your
web application's message: "Hello from Kubernetes on your local
cluster!"

4.6. Step 5: Testing and Troubleshooting

It's normal to encounter a few bumps along the way. Here are a few
tips if something doesn't work as expected:

- **Checking Logs:**
  If your application isn't behaving correctly, check the logs of the Pods:

bash

```
kubectl logs <pod-name>
```

- **Describing Resources:**
  Get more detailed information by describing the Pod or Deployment:

bash

```
kubectl describe pod <pod-name>
```

- **Restarting the Cluster:**
  If you encounter persistent issues, consider restarting your Minikube cluster:

bash

```
minikube stop
minikube start
```

- **Verifying Docker Image:**
  Ensure that your Docker image was built correctly and is tagged properly. You might need to re-build the image if changes were made.

4.7. Wrapping Up the Project

After testing, it's a good idea to clean up your environment. Delete the deployment and service to keep your local cluster organized:

bash

```
kubectl delete -f service.yaml
kubectl delete -f deployment.yaml
```

This project has taken you through the complete cycle: from creating an application, containerizing it, and then deploying it on your local

Kubernetes cluster. Each step was designed to be easy to follow, with clear instructions and practical examples. The skills you've developed here are directly applicable in many real-world scenarios, whether you work in healthcare, manufacturing, logistics, or any field where scalable, efficient applications are needed.

---

5. Additional Tips and Best Practices

Working with Kubernetes may seem challenging at first, but with steady practice, you'll build confidence. Here are a few extra tips to help you along the way:

5.1. Experimentation and Learning

- **Practice Regularly:**
  Spend time in your local environment experimenting with different configurations and commands. Every experiment, successful or not, teaches you something valuable.

- **Ask Questions:**
  There are many online communities and forums dedicated to Kubernetes. If you encounter a problem, chances are someone else has too. Use these resources to gain insights and practical advice.

- **Document Your Process:**
  Keep notes on the commands you run and the configurations you change. This record can be a valuable reference as you work on more complex projects.

5.2. Real-World Considerations

- **Resource Management:**
  In a production environment, keeping an eye on resource usage (CPU, memory, storage) is critical. Familiarize yourself with Kubernetes commands that show resource utilization.

- **Security Practices:**
  While your local setup is safe for learning, remember that real deployments need proper security measures. As you progress, look into role-based access control (RBAC) and network policies.

- **Scalability and Redundancy:**
  Practice scaling your deployments and testing the resilience of your applications. Understanding how Kubernetes manages load and recovers from failures is key for real-world applications.

5.3. Building on This Knowledge

The skills you gain from this chapter set a strong foundation. Here are some ideas for next steps:

- **Extend Your Application:**
  Add more routes or features to your Flask application. Experiment with adding a database or connecting multiple services.

- **Explore Advanced Configurations:**
  Look into ConfigMaps and Secrets to manage configuration data and sensitive information in your deployments.

- **Integrate Continuous Deployment:**
  Once you're comfortable with deployments, explore integrating CI/CD pipelines to automate the build and deployment process.

5.4. Encouragement for Beginners

Starting with Kubernetes can be overwhelming, but every expert started exactly where you are now. The key is to keep trying, practice regularly, and learn from each step. Your local environment is your testing ground—a safe space to build and refine your skills. Don't be discouraged by initial setbacks; troubleshooting is part of the learning process. Every error you encounter is a step toward deeper understanding.

6. Recap and Final Thoughts

Let's summarize what you've learned in this chapter:

- **Installing and Configuring a Local Environment:**
  You installed Docker, Minikube, and kubectl, creating a robust environment for experimentation.

- **Understanding Key Components:**
  You learned about Pods, Nodes, Clusters, and Services—the building blocks of Kubernetes.

- **Creating Your First Pod:**
  You wrote a basic YAML configuration to create a Pod and deployed it using kubectl.

- **Running a Simple Application:**
  Through a hands-on project, you containerized a simple Flask application, deployed it to your local cluster, and accessed it via a NodePort service.

As you review these topics, you should feel more comfortable with the basics of Kubernetes. Each concept builds upon the previous one, giving you a clear path to managing containerized applications effectively. The practical projects in this chapter were designed to be accessible and to provide a strong foundation that you can expand on in future chapters.

Your local Kubernetes cluster is now a powerful tool that you can use to test new ideas, simulate real-world deployments, and experiment with various configurations. Keep exploring and experimenting. The more you work with these tools, the more natural they will become.

Remember that practice is key. Take some time after this chapter to repeat some of the exercises. Try modifying the YAML files, experiment with different Docker images, or even scale your deployments. Every change you make is a step forward in understanding how Kubernetes manages applications.

---

7. Hands-on Exercises and Challenges

To reinforce what you've learned, here are some additional exercises you can try on your own:

7.1. Exercise 1: Modify the First Pod

- **Task:**
  Edit your first-pod.yaml to include an environment variable that your container prints on startup.

- **Steps:**
  Add an env section under the container specification. Then modify the container command to echo the environment variable's value.

- **Expected Outcome:**
  When you deploy the updated Pod, the logs should show the value of the environment variable.

7.2. Exercise 2: Scale Your Deployment

- **Task:**
  Change the number of replicas in your deployment.yaml from 2 to 4.

- **Steps:**
  Edit the file, apply the changes, and then use kubectl get pods to confirm that four Pods are running.

- **Expected Outcome:**
  You will see additional Pods being created and managed by Kubernetes.

7.3. Exercise 3: Experiment with Different Container Images

- **Task:**
  Instead of using the busybox image for your first Pod, try using another lightweight image such as Alpine Linux.

- **Steps:**
  Modify your YAML file to replace the image and apply the changes. Monitor the logs to see if the new image works as expected.

- **Expected Outcome:**
  The Pod should run using the new image with similar behavior.

7.4. Exercise 4: Explore Pod Networking

- **Task:**
  Create two Pods that run a simple server application and another Pod that acts as a client to communicate with the server.

- **Steps:**
  Write separate YAML files for the server and client Pods. Use labels and Services to enable communication.

- **Expected Outcome:**
  The client Pod should be able to connect to the server Pod through the Service.

These exercises are designed to be practical. They mirror challenges faced in real-world applications, where you might need to adjust configurations on the fly, scale services, or troubleshoot networking issues. As you work through these challenges, you will gain hands-on experience that is directly applicable in various industries like manufacturing, healthcare, and logistics.

8. Final Words

By now, you have a solid understanding of how to set up and use a local Kubernetes environment. You've learned the basics of Kubernetes architecture and have had hands-on practice by creating Pods and deploying a simple application. These early experiences are the building blocks for more advanced topics, and the skills you develop here will support your future endeavors in container orchestration.

Take pride in the progress you've made. With every command executed and configuration applied, you're building the skills necessary to work with Kubernetes in real-world scenarios. Whether your goal is to deploy scalable applications or to manage complex systems in a production environment, the foundation you have now is a valuable asset.

As you move on to the next chapters, keep experimenting, learning, and refining your approach. Each new project will present fresh challenges and opportunities to grow. Always remember that persistence and hands-on practice are key to mastering any technology.

Keep this chapter handy as you work through additional exercises and projects. Review the concepts when needed, and don't hesitate to revisit your configuration files to see how changes affect your cluster's behavior. The learning process is ongoing, and every experiment makes you more confident in your abilities.

Thank you for taking the time to work through this material. Your journey into Kubernetes is just beginning, and the skills you develop here will serve you well in your career and personal projects. Enjoy the process, ask questions when you're stuck, and remember—you have the power to control your own learning. You can do it!

CHAPTER 3: CORE CONCEPTS AND ARCHITECTURE

Welcome to this chapter on the core concepts and architecture of Kubernetes. Here, we will explore the fundamental building blocks that make Kubernetes function the way it does. By breaking down the control plane, nodes, and networking within a cluster, you will gain a clear picture of how all the components work together. We will use a relatable workshop analogy to explain how these pieces fit in a practical setting. Plus, there's a hands-on project at the end to help you put these ideas into practice. If you're ready to roll up your sleeves and get into the details, let's begin.

---

1. Understanding the Kubernetes Control Plane

The control plane is the brain of a Kubernetes cluster. It manages all the decisions regarding scheduling, scaling, and responding to cluster events. Even though it works behind the scenes, knowing how it functions is essential for anyone working with Kubernetes.

1.1. What the Control Plane Does

Think of the control plane as a central command center that keeps track of what needs to be done, where it should happen, and how to handle issues if something goes wrong. It maintains a real-time snapshot of the entire cluster, ensuring that the desired state you declare matches the actual state running on your nodes.

1.2. Key Components of the Control Plane

Let's break down the main parts of the control plane:

- **API Server:**
  The API server is the interface for all communication with the cluster. Whether you're using the command-line tool or interacting through an application, your commands go through the API server. It validates and processes API requests and updates the cluster state accordingly.

- **Scheduler:**
  The scheduler is responsible for assigning Pods to nodes. It looks at the available resources and other constraints to decide where a new Pod should run. Think of it as someone who carefully decides which workstation in a busy office should handle a new task.

- **Controller Manager:**
  This component runs a set of controllers that monitor the cluster. These controllers continuously work to ensure that the cluster's actual state matches your desired state. For example, if you've requested three replicas of an application, the controller manager makes sure that there are always three Pods running.

- **etcd:**
  A distributed key-value store used to persist the cluster's state. It is the memory bank for your Kubernetes cluster, keeping all the configuration data and status information.

1.3. How the Control Plane Operates

Imagine a large company office with a central operations center. Every decision, from which projects need additional resources to how work should be divided among teams, goes through this hub. In Kubernetes, the control plane continuously monitors the state of the cluster and makes adjustments if something goes off track.

Hands-On Exploration: Interacting with the Control Plane

You can explore the control plane with a few simple commands using **kubectl**. For example, running the command below gives you an overview of the nodes and their status:

bash

```
kubectl get nodes
```
Try describing a node to see more detailed information:

bash

```
kubectl describe node <node-name>
```
Reviewing these outputs can provide insight into how the control plane distributes work and maintains order in your cluster. Experiment with different commands to see how your cluster responds to changes.

2. Nodes and Worker Components

The worker nodes are the workhorses of the cluster. They are where your applications actually run. Each node is like a workstation equipped with all the necessary tools to execute the tasks assigned by the control plane.

2.1. What is a Node?

A node is a machine—either physical or virtual—that runs the containerized applications. Every node is managed by the control plane and has a set of components that help it perform its duties.

2.2. Key Components on a Node

- **Kubelet:**
  The kubelet is an agent that runs on every node. It listens to the control plane and ensures that the containers running on the node match the desired specifications. If a container fails or isn't running as expected, the kubelet takes action to remedy the situation.

- **Container Runtime:**
  This is the software that is responsible for running containers. Docker is one popular option, but there are other runtimes available. The container runtime pulls images from a registry, starts and stops containers, and handles the container lifecycle.

- **Kube-proxy:**
  Kube-proxy handles network communication for the node. It ensures that network traffic is correctly routed to the appropriate container. Kube-proxy is crucial for the functioning of services in your cluster.

2.3. How Nodes Work Together

Imagine a workshop with several workstations. Each workstation is equipped with specific tools (kubelet, container runtime, and kube-proxy) and follows instructions from the manager (the control plane). When a new task is issued, each workstation takes on its share of the work, ensuring that the overall production line runs smoothly.

Hands-On Exploration: Checking Node Details

To see how your nodes are performing, use the following command:

bash

```
kubectl get nodes
```
You can then inspect a particular node with:

bash

```
kubectl describe node <node-name>
```
This command provides details such as available resources, running processes, and network information. Experiment with these commands to build your comfort level in managing nodes.

---

3. Networking Basics Within a Kubernetes Cluster

Networking in Kubernetes is a complex but essential subject. It ensures that all components in the cluster can communicate with each other seamlessly, even as they run on different nodes.

3.1. Pod Networking

Every Pod in Kubernetes gets its own IP address. This setup means that containers within a Pod can communicate with each other using localhost, while different Pods communicate over the network using their assigned IPs. This design simplifies communication and isolation between applications.

3.2. Service Networking

Services provide a stable endpoint for accessing a set of Pods. Even if the underlying Pods change, the service's IP address remains the same. This consistency is critical for applications that need to be accessible both inside and outside the cluster.

3.3. Network Policies

Network policies allow you to control traffic between Pods. They define how groups of Pods can communicate with each other, which is important for maintaining security and efficient network use. While network policies can get detailed, the basic idea is to set rules for who can talk to whom.

Hands-On Exploration: Testing Pod Connectivity

A simple way to explore networking is by creating two Pods and checking if they can talk to each other. For example, you can deploy one Pod that acts as a web server and another as a client. Then, use tools like curl to send a request from the client Pod to the server Pod.

Create a basic server Pod using a simple HTTP server image. Then, in a client Pod, run a command like:

bash

```
curl http://<server-pod-ip>:<port>
```
This command will help you see how traffic flows within your cluster. Tinkering with network policies in a controlled setting is a great way to understand their impact.

4. Real-World Analogy: A Busy Workshop

To make all these technical components more relatable, let's compare a Kubernetes cluster to a bustling workshop. Think of the entire cluster as a workshop with different stations where each station has a specific role. This analogy can help bring clarity to how the control plane, nodes, and networking work together.

4.1. The Workshop Manager (Control Plane)

At the heart of the workshop is the manager. This person oversees the entire operation, makes sure every task is assigned to the right station, and ensures that all parts of the workshop work in harmony. The manager monitors the workflow and makes adjustments when a station is overloaded or underperforming.

- The API server is the communication hub where instructions are passed from the manager to the workstations.

- The scheduler reviews the work to be done and decides which station (node) will handle each task.

- The controller manager keeps an eye on the output and ensures that the workshop runs as planned.

- The key-value store (etcd) serves as the workshop's ledger, keeping records of all ongoing tasks and configurations.

4.2. The Workstations (Nodes)

Each workstation in the workshop is equipped with tools and equipment to complete assigned tasks. In a Kubernetes cluster, these workstations are the nodes. Every node has its own set of tools (kubelet, container runtime, kube-proxy) that allow it to perform tasks efficiently.

- The kubelet ensures that each task is carried out as instructed.

- The container runtime is like the machinery that runs the processes.

- The kube-proxy is responsible for making sure that any communication, whether between workstations or with the outside world, is routed correctly.

4.3. Communication in the Workshop (Networking)

In a busy workshop, clear and efficient communication is crucial. Think of the networking in Kubernetes as the channels through which workers communicate. Each workstation (or Pod) has a dedicated line of communication (IP address) and the workshop has a central board (Services) that routes requests to the appropriate station.

- Pods communicate with one another directly using their private lines.

- Services ensure that no matter how the workstations (Pods) change over time, there is always a stable way to contact them.

- Network policies are like the rules in a workshop that determine who can speak with whom, ensuring that sensitive or critical operations are not disrupted by unwanted interference.

5. Hands-On Project: Building Your Own Workshop Simulation

Now that we have explored the core concepts and built a clear analogy of how a Kubernetes cluster functions, it's time to put your knowledge to work. In this project, you will simulate a workshop by deploying several Pods that act as different workstations and then creating a service to coordinate their activities. This practical project will reinforce your understanding of the control plane, nodes, and networking.

5.1. Project Overview

In this project, we will:

- Deploy multiple Pods that represent different stations in a workshop.

- Create a service that acts as the central communication hub.

- Verify that the Pods can communicate with each other and with the service.

5.2. Step-by-Step Instructions

Step 1: Prepare Your Environment

Ensure that your local Kubernetes cluster is running. If you're using Minikube, start it with:

bash

minikube start

Confirm that your cluster is active with:

bash

kubectl get nodes

Step 2: Create Pod Configurations for Workstations

Create a new directory for your project:

bash

```
mkdir workshop-simulation
cd workshop-simulation
```

Inside this directory, create a file named station-pod.yaml with the following content. This file will be used to deploy multiple Pods that simulate workstations:

yaml

```
apiVersion: v1
kind: Pod
metadata:
  name: station-1
  labels:
    role: workstation
spec:
  containers:
  - name: station-container
    image: busybox
    command: ["sh", "-c", "echo 'Station 1 is active'; sleep 3600"]
---
apiVersion: v1
kind: Pod
metadata:
  name: station-2
  labels:
    role: workstation
spec:
  containers:
  - name: station-container
    image: busybox
    command: ["sh", "-c", "echo 'Station 2 is active'; sleep 3600"]
```

Feel free to add more stations by following the same pattern. Each Pod simulates a workstation with a simple command that prints a message and then sleeps.

Apply the configuration:

bash

```
kubectl apply -f station-pod.yaml
```
Verify the Pods are running:

bash

```
kubectl get pods -l role=workstation
```
Step 3: Create a Service for the Workshop

Now, create a service that will act as the central hub for these stations. Create a file named workshop-service.yaml with the following content:

yaml

```
apiVersion: v1
kind: Service
metadata:
  name: workshop-service
spec:
  selector:
    role: workstation
  ports:
  - protocol: TCP
    port: 80
    targetPort: 8080
  type: NodePort
```
In this file, the service selects all Pods labeled as workstations and exposes them on port 80, mapping it to a target port on the Pods. (If you want to simulate different ports, adjust the configuration accordingly.)

Apply the service configuration:

bash

```
kubectl apply -f workshop-service.yaml
```
Step 4: Verify Communication

Once the service is running, check that you can access it from within the cluster. You can create a temporary Pod to test connectivity:

bash

```
kubectl run test-client --image=busybox -it --rm -- sh
```
Inside the test-client Pod, try to ping the service:

bash

```
wget -qO- http://workshop-service
```
If everything is set up correctly, you should see a response indicating that one of your station Pods is active.

Step 5: Experiment and Expand

Now that your workshop simulation is running, consider experimenting with the setup:

- **Scale Up the Number of Stations:**
  Edit your YAML file to add more Pods simulating additional workstations.

- **Modify the Commands:**
  Change the commands in the Pods to simulate different tasks or roles within the workshop.

- **Test Network Policies:**
  Introduce network policies to restrict communication between stations and see how the traffic is affected.

This project gives you a hands-on opportunity to understand how a Kubernetes cluster manages multiple components and how they work together to process tasks.

6. Troubleshooting and Best Practices

As you work through your projects, you might encounter challenges. Here are some practical tips to help you overcome common issues:

6.1. Monitoring and Logs

- **Use Kubectl Logs:**
  To check what's happening inside a Pod, run:

bash

kubectl logs <pod-name>
Logs can provide insight into errors or misconfigurations.

- **Describe Commands:**
  If a Pod is not behaving as expected, use:

bash

kubectl describe pod <pod-name>
This command shows detailed information about the Pod, including recent events.

6.2. Checking Resource Allocation

Sometimes, issues may arise from insufficient resources. Use the following commands to check resource usage on your nodes:

bash

kubectl top nodes
kubectl top pods
These commands can help you decide whether you need to adjust resource limits or scale your cluster.

6.3. Clean-Up Procedures

When you finish testing your projects, it's good practice to clean up the resources to keep your environment tidy. Use commands like:

bash

```
kubectl delete -f station-pod.yaml
kubectl delete -f workshop-service.yaml
```

Regular clean-up helps avoid clutter and ensures that your local cluster remains responsive.

---

7. Recap of Key Concepts

Let's take a moment to review the main points we've covered in this chapter:

- **Control Plane:**
  Acts as the central command center managing the state and operations of the cluster. It includes the API server, scheduler, controller manager, and the key-value store.

- **Nodes and Worker Components:**
  Nodes are the machines where your applications run. Each node includes tools like the kubelet, container runtime, and kube-proxy, all of which ensure that your tasks are executed as expected.

- **Networking in Kubernetes:**
  Networking ensures that every component, whether a Pod or a Service, can communicate reliably. Pod networking, Service networking, and network policies work together to manage the flow of data within the cluster.

- **Workshop Analogy:**
  We compared the cluster to a busy workshop where the control plane is the manager, nodes are the workstations, and the network is the communication system that connects everything together.

- **Hands-On Project:**
  You created a simulation where multiple Pods represented different workstations and a central service coordinated their actions. This project not only solidified your understanding but also provided a practical example of how Kubernetes components work together.

---

8. Additional Exercises to Enhance Your Skills

To build on what you've learned, here are some additional exercises:

Exercise 1: Enhance the Control Plane Interaction

- **Task:**
  Use additional kubectl commands to inspect and interact with the control plane. For example, try listing all available API resources:

bash

kubectl api-resources

- **Challenge:**
  Identify a few resources and use kubectl explain to read their documentation.

Exercise 2: Expand the Workshop Simulation

- **Task:**
  Modify your simulation to include a Pod that simulates an "inspection station" responsible for monitoring the status of other stations.

- **Challenge:**
  Create a separate YAML file for this new station and add a Service that routes inspection data. Use simple commands inside the Pod to print status messages.

Exercise 3: Test Network Isolation

- **Task:**
  Introduce a basic network policy that restricts communication between Pods with different labels.

- **Challenge:**
  Create a YAML file for a network policy that allows traffic only between Pods labeled as workstations, then test by deploying Pods with different labels.

---

9. Final Thoughts and Next Steps

You have now explored the core concepts and architecture that underpin Kubernetes. With a firm grasp of how the control plane manages the cluster, how nodes operate as workstations, and how networking brings everything together, you are well prepared to move on to more advanced topics. The workshop analogy should serve as a mental model to remind you that every part of the system works together to keep things running smoothly.

As you progress, keep experimenting with the projects and exercises provided. Adjust configurations, add new components, and see how your changes affect the overall behavior of the cluster. Each experiment is a step toward mastering these technologies, and every challenge you encounter will help build your confidence.

Remember, the key to success with Kubernetes is practice and persistence. Use your local cluster as a testing ground for new ideas. Over time, the commands and configurations will become second nature, and you'll be able to tackle more complex deployments with ease.

This chapter has provided a comprehensive overview of the Kubernetes control plane, nodes, and networking, along with a hands-on project to solidify your understanding. Use the skills you've gained here as the foundation for future projects, whether they involve scaling applications, integrating with continuous deployment pipelines, or securing complex systems in a production environment.

Take a break, review the material, and come back with fresh ideas for further experimentation. You are building a solid base of knowledge that will serve you in many practical, real-world scenarios. Keep testing, keep learning, and remember—you can handle any challenge that comes your way.

CHAPTER 4: DEPLOYMENTS AND SCALING

Welcome to the chapter on Deployments and Scaling in Kubernetes! In this chapter, we'll explore how Kubernetes manages the rollout of your applications and the strategies you can use to adjust to changing loads. We'll cover the following key topics:

- **How Deployments Work in Kubernetes**

- **Managing Rolling Updates and Rollbacks**

- **Hands-on Project: Deploying a Multi-Tier Application**

- **Scaling: Horizontal vs. Vertical Scaling and When to Use Each Approach**

Our goal is to break down these concepts into clear, actionable steps using everyday analogies and relatable examples. Whether you're new to Kubernetes or looking to expand your skills, you'll find plenty of practical guidance to help you along the way. Let's jump right in!

---

1. Understanding Deployments in Kubernetes

Imagine you run a small business that frequently updates its menu. Each time you change your offerings, you want the changes to be smooth and uninterrupted. In the world of Kubernetes, a **Deployment** is like the process of updating your menu while ensuring that your customers always have something to enjoy. Deployments handle the creation, updating, and scaling of Pods, ensuring that your desired state is maintained without downtime.

1.1. What is a Deployment?

A Deployment in Kubernetes is a resource that defines how an application should be run. It describes the desired state of the application, such as the number of replicas, the container image to use, and any specific configurations. Once you create a Deployment, Kubernetes takes over and makes sure that the actual state of your cluster matches this desired state.

Key Points:

- **Declarative Nature:**
  You declare what you want in a YAML file, and Kubernetes makes it happen.

- **Self-Healing:**
  If a Pod goes down, the Deployment controller creates a new one to replace it.

- **Version Control:**
  Deployments allow you to manage different versions of your application, which is handy when you need to update or revert changes.

1.2. How Does a Deployment Work?

Think of a Deployment like a recipe for a favorite dish. You specify the ingredients (container images, environment variables, etc.) and the number of servings (replicas). The chef (Kubernetes) follows the recipe to prepare the dish, and if something isn't quite right, the chef makes adjustments to ensure the dish meets your expectations.

When you apply a Deployment configuration:

1. **Creation:**
   Kubernetes creates Pods as specified.

2. **Monitoring:**
   It continually monitors these Pods to ensure they remain in the desired state.

3. **Updates:**
   When you update the Deployment, Kubernetes gradually replaces the old Pods with new ones, ensuring there's no interruption in service.

1.3. Deployment Strategies

There are several strategies you can choose from when rolling out a new version of your application:

- **Rolling Updates:**
  This is the default strategy. New Pods are created gradually while old Pods are terminated. It ensures that a certain number of Pods are always available.

- **Blue/Green Deployments:**
  In this strategy, you maintain two separate environments— one for the current version (blue) and one for the new version (green). Once the new version is tested and verified, traffic is switched over to green.

- **Canary Deployments:**
  You release the new version to a small subset of users first.

This way, you can monitor performance and catch any issues before rolling it out to everyone.

Each strategy has its advantages and trade-offs. For example, rolling updates provide a smooth transition with minimal disruption, while canary deployments allow you to test the waters with a smaller group of users.

---

2. Managing Rolling Updates and Rollbacks

Updates are a part of software development, but they need to be managed carefully to avoid downtime or performance issues. Rolling updates let you update your application gradually, ensuring that there is always a working version running. And if something goes wrong, rollbacks let you revert to the previous stable version.

2.1. Rolling Updates Explained

Picture a busy highway where lanes are slowly closed for maintenance. Instead of shutting down the entire road at once, workers close one lane at a time, rerouting traffic while keeping the highway open. Rolling updates work in a similar fashion:

- **Gradual Replacement:**
  Kubernetes replaces Pods one at a time (or in small batches), ensuring that there's always a set of Pods available to serve users.

- **Zero Downtime:**
  Because not all Pods are replaced simultaneously, users experience a seamless transition from the old version to the new one.

- **Monitoring:**
  The Deployment controller monitors each new Pod as it comes online. If any issues are detected, it can pause the update process.

Hands-On Tip:

To perform a rolling update, modify the container image in your Deployment YAML file and apply the changes. For example:

yaml

```
spec:
 template:
  spec:
   containers:
   - name: web-app
     image: my-app:v2
```
Apply the update with:

bash

```
kubectl apply -f deployment.yaml
```
Kubernetes then gradually replaces the old Pods with new ones running the updated image.

2.2. Rollbacks: Going Back to Safety

Sometimes, even the best plans run into trouble. Maybe the new version has a bug or performance issue. With rollbacks, you can revert to the previous version of your application quickly. Kubernetes maintains a history of changes for Deployments, allowing you to roll back if needed.

How to Roll Back:

1. **Check the Rollout History:**
   Use the following command to see previous revisions:

```
bash
```

kubectl rollout history deployment/<deployment-name>

2. **Perform a Rollback:**

   Roll back to the previous version by running:

```
bash
```

kubectl rollout undo deployment/<deployment-name>

3. **Monitor the Rollback:**

   After initiating the rollback, monitor the status to ensure that the previous version is restored correctly.

2.3. Real-World Example: Software Update in a Retail Store

Imagine a retail store updating its checkout system. The store doesn't shut down all registers at once; instead, it updates one register at a time. If the new system causes issues, the store can revert that single register to the old system while investigating the problem. This minimizes customer impact and keeps operations running smoothly. Rolling updates and rollbacks in Kubernetes work on a similar principle.

---

3. Hands-on Project: Deploying a Multi-Tier Application

Now that you understand how Deployments work and how to manage updates and rollbacks, let's put this knowledge into practice with a hands-on project. In this project, you will deploy a multi-tier web application that consists of a frontend, backend, and database layer. This will demonstrate how Kubernetes manages complex applications with multiple components that need to work in harmony.

3.1. Project Overview

In this project, we will:

- Create and configure Deployments for a multi-tier application.

- Set up a Service for each tier to manage communication.

- Test rolling updates and perform a rollback if necessary.

- Explore horizontal scaling by adjusting the number of replicas.

Imagine your application as a restaurant:

- The **frontend** is the dining area where customers interact.

- The **backend** is the kitchen where orders are processed.

- The **database** is the pantry that stores all the ingredients and recipes.

Each component needs to work together seamlessly, and Kubernetes ensures that even if one part of the restaurant needs an update, the whole system continues to function.

3.2. Step 1: Preparing Your Application Components

Frontend (Dining Area)

We'll start by deploying a simple web server for the frontend. Create a file called frontend-deployment.yaml with the following content:

yaml

```yaml
apiVersion: apps/v1
kind: Deployment
metadata:
  name: frontend-deployment
  labels:
    tier: frontend
spec:
  replicas: 2
  selector:
    matchLabels:
      tier: frontend
  template:
    metadata:
      labels:
        tier: frontend
    spec:
      containers:
      - name: frontend
        image: nginx:alpine
        ports:
        - containerPort: 80
```

Create a corresponding Service file, frontend-service.yaml, to expose the frontend:

yaml

```yaml
apiVersion: v1
kind: Service
metadata:
  name: frontend-service
spec:
  type: NodePort
  selector:
    tier: frontend
  ports:
  - port: 80
    targetPort: 80
```

    nodePort: 30080

Backend (Kitchen)

Next, create a Deployment for the backend. Create a file called backend-deployment.yaml with the following content:

yaml

```
apiVersion: apps/v1
kind: Deployment
metadata:
 name: backend-deployment
 labels:
  tier: backend
spec:
 replicas: 2
 selector:
  matchLabels:
   tier: backend
 template:
  metadata:
   labels:
    tier: backend
  spec:
   containers:
   - name: backend
     image: hashicorp/http-echo
     args:
     - "-text=Hello from the backend!"
     ports:
     - containerPort: 5678
```

Then, create a Service for the backend, backend-service.yaml:

yaml

```
apiVersion: v1
kind: Service
metadata:
 name: backend-service
spec:
 selector:
  tier: backend
```

```
  ports:
  - port: 80
    targetPort: 5678
  type: ClusterIP
```

Database (Pantry)

For the database, we can simulate a simple storage component using a lightweight database image. Create database-deployment.yaml:

yaml

```
apiVersion: apps/v1
kind: Deployment
metadata:
  name: database-deployment
  labels:
    tier: database
spec:
  replicas: 1
  selector:
    matchLabels:
      tier: database
  template:
    metadata:
      labels:
        tier: database
    spec:
      containers:
      - name: database
        image: redis:alpine
        ports:
        - containerPort: 6379
```

And a corresponding Service, database-service.yaml:

yaml

```
apiVersion: v1
kind: Service
metadata:
  name: database-service
spec:
```

```
selector:
  tier: database
ports:
- port: 6379
  targetPort: 6379
type: ClusterIP
```

3.3. Step 2: Deploying the Multi-Tier Application

Now that you have the configuration files ready, deploy each component using kubectl.

1. Deploy Frontend:

bash

```
kubectl apply -f frontend-deployment.yaml
kubectl apply -f frontend-service.yaml
```

2. Deploy Backend:

bash

```
kubectl apply -f backend-deployment.yaml
kubectl apply -f backend-service.yaml
```

3. Deploy Database:

bash

```
kubectl apply -f database-deployment.yaml
kubectl apply -f database-service.yaml
```

After applying these configurations, verify that all Deployments are running:

bash
```
kubectl get deployments
kubectl get pods
```
You should see your frontend, backend, and database Pods running.

3.4. Step 3: Testing and Performing a Rolling Update

Now that your multi-tier application is deployed, it's time to test a rolling update. Let's update the backend to display a different message.

1. **Modify the Backend Deployment:** Open backend-deployment.yaml and change the argument for the container:

yaml

```
args:
- "-text=New update: Backend is updated!"
```

2. **Apply the Update:**

bash

```
kubectl apply -f backend-deployment.yaml
```

3. **Monitor the Rolling Update:** Check the rollout status:

bash

```
kubectl rollout status deployment/backend-deployment
```

Kubernetes will replace the old backend Pods gradually. You can inspect the Pods:

bash

```
kubectl get pods -l tier=backend
```

Performing a Rollback:

If you notice any issues with the update, revert to the previous version:

bash

```
kubectl rollout undo deployment/backend-deployment
```

This command rolls back the Deployment to the previous stable state.

3.5. Step 4: Scaling Your Application

Scaling is the process of adjusting the number of replicas for a Deployment to handle changes in load. There are two main approaches:

Horizontal Scaling (Scaling Out):

- **Definition:**
  Increasing or decreasing the number of Pods.

- **When to Use:**
  When your application experiences variable load, horizontal scaling helps distribute traffic evenly.

- **How to Do It:**
  Modify the replicas field in your Deployment YAML file or use the command:

bash

```
kubectl scale deployment/frontend-deployment --replicas=4
```

Vertical Scaling (Scaling Up):

- **Definition:**
  Adjusting the resources (CPU, memory) allocated to each Pod.

- **When to Use:**
  When a Pod needs more resources to handle increased demand, but scaling out is not feasible.

- **How to Do It:**
  Modify the resource requests and limits in the Pod specification:

yaml

```
resources:
 requests:
   memory: "64Mi"
   cpu: "250m"
 limits:
   memory: "128Mi"
   cpu: "500m"
```
Then apply the updated configuration.

Hands-On Scaling Example:

Try scaling your frontend Deployment to see how the cluster handles increased load:

1. **Scale Out:**

bash

```
kubectl scale deployment/frontend-deployment --replicas=4
```
2. **Verify the Change:**

bash

```
kubectl get pods -l tier=frontend
```
3. **Scale Back Down:** Once you've observed the change, you can revert to the original replica count:

bash

```
kubectl scale deployment/frontend-deployment --replicas=2
```

---

4. Real-World Analogies and Insights

To make these concepts even more relatable, let's compare your application to a popular real-world scenario: a restaurant with different departments and shifts.

4.1. Restaurant Update and Scaling Analogy

Imagine you own a restaurant that occasionally updates its menu (rolling updates). The kitchen staff (backend) prepares the dishes, the waiters (frontend) serve customers, and the pantry (database) supplies ingredients. Here's how our Kubernetes concepts map to this scenario:

- **Deployments:**
  Like the restaurant's management plan, a Deployment ensures that a certain number of staff are always on duty and ready to serve. When you update the menu, you want the new dishes to be prepared while still serving customers—this is the rolling update process.

- **Rolling Updates:**
  Instead of firing all staff and hiring new ones at once, you gradually introduce the new team. This way, customers experience minimal disruption. If a new dish isn't well received, you can quickly revert to the old menu (rollback).

- **Scaling:**
  On busy nights, you might hire additional waiters and kitchen staff (horizontal scaling) to handle increased demand. Alternatively, you might invest in better equipment that allows your current staff to work faster (vertical scaling). Kubernetes lets you adjust the number of Pods or the resources allocated to them, similar to these decisions in a restaurant.

4.2. Practical Takeaways

- **Plan for Growth:**
  Whether it's a restaurant or a web application, planning for

increased demand is crucial. Kubernetes makes it easy to scale applications without downtime.

- **Monitor and Adjust:**
  Keep an eye on performance. Use Kubernetes commands to monitor the status of your Deployments, and adjust replicas or resource allocations as needed.

- **Embrace Flexibility:**
  Updates and changes are part of life. With Kubernetes, you can roll out changes gradually and quickly revert if necessary.

---

5. Additional Exercises and Best Practices

Now that you've seen Deployments and Scaling in action, here are some extra exercises to reinforce your learning:

Exercise 1: Experiment with Canary Deployments

- **Task:**
  Set up a new Deployment that introduces a new version of your backend. Instead of updating all Pods at once, deploy one or two Pods with the new version while keeping the rest unchanged.

- **Steps:**

  - Create a new Deployment file for the canary release.

  - Use labels to distinguish between the canary and stable versions.

o   Monitor performance and test the new version before a full rollout.

Exercise 2: Implement Auto-Scaling

- **Task:**
  Learn about Kubernetes' Horizontal Pod Autoscaler (HPA) to automatically adjust the number of replicas based on CPU usage.

- **Steps:**

  o   Enable metrics-server in your cluster if it's not already running.

  o   Create an HPA for one of your Deployments:

bash

```
kubectl autoscale deployment backend-deployment --cpu-percent=50 --min=2 --max=6
```
Monitor the autoscaler behavior using:

bash

```
kubectl get hpa
```
- **Expected Outcome:**
  The HPA should adjust the number of Pods based on the load, providing a practical example of dynamic scaling.

Exercise 3: Resource Tuning for Vertical Scaling

- **Task:**
  Modify one of your Deployment configurations to adjust resource requests and limits. Observe how the change affects the Pod's performance.

- **Steps:**

o   Update the resource section in your YAML file.

o   Apply the changes and use:

bash

kubectl describe pod <pod-name>
to see the updated resource allocation.

- **Expected Outcome:**
  You'll learn how to fine-tune your application's performance by allocating more (or fewer) resources.

Best Practices

- **Use Version Control:**
  Always version your Deployment configurations using Git or another version control system. This way, you can track changes and roll back easily if something goes wrong.

- **Regularly Monitor Deployments:**
  Get into the habit of checking your deployments and Pods frequently. Tools like kubectl get pods, kubectl describe, and monitoring dashboards can help you spot issues before they escalate.

- **Document Your Changes:**
  Maintain a change log for updates and scaling operations. This documentation is invaluable for troubleshooting and planning future deployments.

- **Test in a Staging Environment:**
  Before applying changes in a production environment, use a staging area to test new configurations. This minimizes the risk of downtime and unexpected behavior.

6. Recap and Key Takeaways

Let's summarize what we've learned in this chapter:

- **Deployments:**
  They allow you to manage the lifecycle of your application Pods. By declaring a desired state, Kubernetes ensures that your application is always running as expected.

- **Rolling Updates:**
  This strategy lets you update your application gradually, ensuring continuous availability. If issues arise, you can use rollbacks to revert to a previous stable version.

- **Scaling:**
  Whether you scale horizontally (adding more Pods) or vertically (increasing resources per Pod), Kubernetes provides the flexibility to handle varying loads. Each method has its appropriate use case based on the nature of your application and the demands placed upon it.

- **Real-World Applications:**
  Using analogies such as restaurant operations, we illustrated how updates and scaling work in a practical context. This understanding is critical whether you're in manufacturing, healthcare, logistics, or any industry where application performance is key.

- **Hands-On Projects:**
  Through the deployment of a multi-tier application, you experienced how to manage a complex application with multiple interconnected components. This project showcased practical deployment, updating, and scaling strategies in a controlled environment.

7. Final Thoughts and Encouragement

Deploying and scaling applications with Kubernetes can transform the way you manage your infrastructure. The techniques we've discussed here not only ensure that your applications remain available during updates, but they also provide the flexibility to adapt to changing demands quickly and efficiently.

It's perfectly normal to feel challenged by these concepts at first. Every expert in Kubernetes started by working through hands-on projects just like this. The key is persistence and continuous experimentation. Don't be afraid to try new things, adjust your configurations, and see what works best for your specific scenario.

Remember, the commands and configurations might seem overwhelming at first, but with time, they become second nature. Use your local cluster as a playground to test out ideas and simulate real-world scenarios. Each experiment, even those that don't work out perfectly, is an opportunity to learn something new.

In the next chapters, we'll explore more advanced topics, including service discovery, persistent storage, and security. But for now, take a moment to appreciate how far you've come. You now understand how to manage application deployments, perform rolling updates, execute rollbacks, and scale your applications both horizontally and vertically.

Keep this chapter as a reference, and don't hesitate to revisit these projects as you build more complex systems. Your journey with Kubernetes is just beginning, and every step you take builds a solid foundation for future success.

You can do this—each command you type, each configuration file you create, is a step toward mastering one of the most powerful tools in modern application deployment and management. Happy coding, and keep pushing your boundaries!

CHAPTER 5: SERVICE DISCOVERY AND LOAD BALANCING

Welcome to this in-depth chapter on Service Discovery and Load Balancing in Kubernetes. In this chapter, we'll explore how to expose your applications, discuss the different types of Services available (ClusterIP, NodePort, and LoadBalancer), and work through a hands-on project that shows you how to create and access services. We'll also talk about real-world challenges, such as handling unexpected load spikes, and offer practical solutions. Whether you're working in manufacturing, healthcare, logistics, or any industry that depends on reliable application performance, this chapter is designed to be both accessible and highly practical.

Our aim is to break down these concepts into manageable pieces using real-world analogies and step-by-step instructions. If you're ready to learn how Kubernetes ensures your applications remain discoverable and available even under heavy load, let's dive right in!

---

1. Exposing Your Applications

Before an application running inside a Kubernetes cluster can be useful to users, it needs to be accessible. In the world of Kubernetes, exposing an application means making it reachable both from within the cluster and externally. Think of it as putting a shop sign on your store so that customers can easily find and enter your business.

1.1. What is Service Discovery?

Service discovery is the process that allows applications to automatically find and communicate with each other within a network. In a Kubernetes cluster, Services play a crucial role in service discovery by creating a stable endpoint that routes traffic to the appropriate Pods. Without service discovery, as Pods are created and destroyed dynamically, it would be nearly impossible to keep track of where an application is running.

Real-World Analogy: The Directory Assistance

Imagine a busy shopping mall where stores open and close frequently. Without a directory, finding a specific store would be chaotic. The mall's directory is like Kubernetes' service discovery: it provides a consistent address (or endpoint) that guides customers (network traffic) to the right store (Pod), regardless of changes happening behind the scenes.

1.2. How Kubernetes Exposes Applications

Kubernetes uses a resource called a **Service** to expose applications. A Service defines a logical set of Pods and a policy to access them. There are several types of Services, and each type is designed for specific scenarios:

- **ClusterIP:**
  The default Service type that exposes the Service on a cluster-internal IP. This means the Service is only reachable from within the cluster.

- **NodePort:**
  Exposes the Service on a static port on each node's IP. This allows external traffic to access the Service through the node's IP address and a specific port.

- **LoadBalancer:**
  Integrates with external load balancers provided by cloud providers. It automatically assigns a public IP to the Service and routes external traffic to the Pods.

---

2. Different Types of Services

Understanding the different types of Services in Kubernetes is essential for determining how best to expose your applications. Let's break down each one.

2.1. ClusterIP: The Internal Connector

The **ClusterIP** Service is the simplest type. It assigns a virtual IP address to a Service that is only reachable within the cluster. This type is ideal for internal communication between different parts of your application.

When to Use ClusterIP:

- For microservices that need to talk to each other within the cluster.

- When you don't require external access to the application.

- To provide a stable internal endpoint regardless of which Pods are serving the request.

Example Scenario:

Consider an internal inventory system in a manufacturing plant. The inventory system's frontend might communicate with a backend service that tracks parts. Both of these components only need to interact within the company's private network, making ClusterIP an ideal choice.

2.2. NodePort: Opening the Door to the Outside World

The **NodePort** Service type exposes your application on a static port on every node in your cluster. This means that the application can be accessed externally by sending requests to any node's IP address at the designated port.

When to Use NodePort:

- For testing purposes when you need to access your application from outside the cluster.

- In small deployments where a load balancer is not available.

- As a stepping stone to more advanced configurations.

Real-World Analogy:

Imagine your company's building has several front doors. Each door (node) has a dedicated doorbell (port). A NodePort Service is like having the same doorbell at every door, so visitors can ring any one of them and still be directed to the right place inside.

2.3. LoadBalancer: Managing Heavy Traffic with Ease

The **LoadBalancer** Service type is used when you want to expose your application to the internet through a cloud provider's load balancer. It automatically creates an external load balancer that distributes incoming traffic across your Pods.

When to Use LoadBalancer:

- For production applications that require high availability.

- When your application is exposed to unpredictable or heavy external traffic.

- To simplify traffic management in cloud environments.

Real-World Analogy:

Think of a LoadBalancer as a dedicated concierge in a high-end hotel. The concierge efficiently directs guests to the appropriate room or service, ensuring that no single service point becomes overwhelmed. Similarly, the LoadBalancer evenly distributes incoming requests to maintain application performance even under heavy load.

---

3. Hands-on Project: Creating and Accessing Services

Now that you understand the different types of Services and how they work, it's time for a hands-on project. In this project, you will create a simple web application, expose it using a Service, and access it from both within and outside the cluster.

3.1. Project Overview

In this project, we will:

- Deploy a simple web application.

- Create a Service to expose the application.

- Verify access to the application from within the cluster and externally.

- Discuss potential issues and how to address them.

Imagine you're setting up a small online shop. The web application is your storefront, and the Service is the sign outside that helps customers find your shop, whether they're walking by or searching online.

3.2. Step 1: Deploying a Simple Web Application

For this project, we will use a basic web server running on Nginx. Follow these steps:

Create a Deployment for the Web Application

1. **Create a Deployment YAML file:** Create a file named web-deployment.yaml with the following content:

yaml

```
apiVersion: apps/v1
kind: Deployment
metadata:
  name: web-deployment
  labels:
    app: simple-web
spec:
  replicas: 2
  selector:
    matchLabels:
      app: simple-web
  template:
    metadata:
      labels:
        app: simple-web
    spec:
      containers:
```

```
- name: nginx-container
  image: nginx:alpine
  ports:
  - containerPort: 80
```

2. **Deploy the Application:** In your terminal, run:

bash

kubectl apply -f web-deployment.yaml

3. **Verify the Deployment:** Check the status of your Pods with:

bash

kubectl get pods -l app=simple-web

3.3. Step 2: Exposing the Application Using a Service

Next, we'll expose the application using a NodePort Service so that it can be accessed externally.

Create a Service YAML file

1. **Create a Service file:** Create a file named web-service.yaml with the following content:

yaml

```
apiVersion: v1
kind: Service
metadata:
  name: web-service
spec:
  selector:
    app: simple-web
  ports:
  - protocol: TCP
    port: 80
    targetPort: 80
    nodePort: 30080
  type: NodePort
```

2. **Deploy the Service:** Run the following command:

bash

```
kubectl apply -f web-service.yaml
```

3. **Verify the Service:** Check that the Service is running by executing:

bash

```
kubectl get service web-service
```

You should see that it is assigned a NodePort (in this case, 30080).

3.4. Step 3: Accessing the Application

Now that the web application is deployed and exposed, you can access it from outside the cluster.

Access from a Web Browser

- Open a web browser and navigate to:

cpp

```
http://<node-ip>:30080
```

Replace <node-ip> with the IP address of any node in your cluster. If you're using Minikube, you can get the IP with:

bash

```
minikube ip
```

Verify Internal Access

- To test service discovery within the cluster, run a temporary Pod:

bash

```
kubectl run curl-pod --image=curlimages/curl -it --rm -- sh
```

- Inside the temporary Pod, run:

```
bash
```

```
curl http://web-service
```
You should see the default Nginx welcome page as output.

3.5. Step 4: Real-World Challenges – Handling Unexpected Load Spikes

Now that you've created and accessed your Service, let's discuss how Kubernetes handles heavy traffic and unexpected load spikes. In real-world applications, sudden increases in traffic can cause performance issues if not properly managed.

Strategies for Handling Load Spikes:

- **Autoscaling:**
  Kubernetes' Horizontal Pod Autoscaler (HPA) can automatically adjust the number of Pods based on resource usage. For example, if CPU usage rises above a certain threshold, HPA can add more replicas to distribute the load.

To set up an autoscaler, ensure that the metrics-server is running in your cluster and then run:

```
bash
```

```
kubectl autoscale deployment web-deployment --cpu-percent=50 --min=2 --max=10
```
This command tells Kubernetes to maintain CPU usage at around 50% by scaling the number of Pods between 2 and 10.

- **Load Balancing Algorithms:**
  The underlying load balancing in cloud environments often uses sophisticated algorithms to distribute traffic evenly across nodes. Kubernetes integrates with these solutions to ensure that no single node gets overwhelmed.

- **Resource Requests and Limits:**
  Defining resource requests and limits for your Pods ensures that each Pod has enough resources and prevents any one Pod from consuming too much of the available capacity.

For example, update your Deployment YAML to include:

yaml

```
resources:
  requests:
    cpu: "250m"
    memory: "64Mi"
  limits:
    cpu: "500m"
    memory: "128Mi"
```

- **Graceful Degradation:**
  In extreme cases, having a strategy to gracefully degrade service—such as serving a static error page or reducing non-critical functionality—can help maintain a basic level of service during peak loads.

Real-World Analogy: Traffic Management in a City

Imagine a city during rush hour. Traffic lights, detours, and dynamic routing are all in place to manage the flow of vehicles. Similarly, Kubernetes' autoscaling and load balancing ensure that application traffic is managed smoothly, even when demand surges unexpectedly. The system adjusts on the fly—adding extra lanes (Pods), rerouting traffic (Service load balancing), and enforcing rules (resource limits) to prevent gridlock.

4. Additional Best Practices and Tips

As you start working with Service Discovery and Load Balancing in Kubernetes, here are some additional tips to keep in mind:

4.1. Use Meaningful Labels and Selectors

Labels are a powerful tool in Kubernetes that allow you to group and identify resources easily. When creating Services, ensure that your labels match those in your Deployments so that the Service can correctly route traffic.

4.2. Monitor and Log

Regular monitoring is essential. Use commands like:

bash

```
kubectl get pods,services
kubectl describe service web-service
```

to understand how your applications are performing. Integrate logging and monitoring tools to keep track of resource usage and traffic patterns.

4.3. Test Under Load

Before moving to production, simulate load using tools like Apache Bench or JMeter. This will help you see how your Services behave under heavy traffic and whether autoscaling kicks in as expected.

4.4. Document Your Configuration

Keep a record of your YAML configurations, autoscaling settings, and any changes you make. Version control these files so that you can roll back to a known good state if needed.

4.5. Plan for Failures

Have strategies in place for when things don't go as planned. Understand how to quickly identify and mitigate issues like misconfigured Services or overloaded nodes.

---

5. Recap and Key Takeaways

Let's review the main points from this chapter:

- **Service Discovery:**
  Kubernetes Services provide a stable endpoint for your applications, making it easy for different components to find and communicate with each other.

- **Types of Services:**

  - **ClusterIP:** Best for internal communication.

  - **NodePort:** Useful for exposing services externally, especially during testing.

  - **LoadBalancer:** Ideal for production environments where you need to manage external traffic.

- **Hands-on Project:**
  We walked through deploying a simple web application, exposing it via a Service, and verifying access both internally and externally.

- **Handling Load Spikes:**
  Autoscaling, load balancing, resource requests, and graceful degradation are strategies to manage unexpected increases in traffic.

- **Real-World Analogies:**
  Comparing Service Discovery and Load Balancing to directory assistance in a mall or traffic management in a city helps ground these abstract concepts in familiar scenarios.

6. Advanced Exercises to Expand Your Skills

To solidify your understanding, here are some additional exercises:

Exercise 1: Experiment with ClusterIP Services

- **Task:**
  Create a ClusterIP Service for an internal application (e.g., a microservice that does not need external access).

- **Steps:**
  Write a YAML file for a ClusterIP Service, apply it, and test internal connectivity using a temporary client Pod.

- **Outcome:**
  You'll learn how to set up services meant only for internal communication and verify that they are not accessible externally.

Exercise 2: Create a Hybrid Environment with Multiple Service Types

- **Task:**
  Deploy two versions of an application—one exposed via NodePort and the other via LoadBalancer.

- **Steps:**
  Create separate YAML files for each Service type, deploy both, and compare how traffic is handled.

- **Outcome:**
  Gain insights into how different Services route traffic and what challenges you might face in a real-world environment.

Exercise 3: Simulate Load Spikes

- **Task:**
  Use a load testing tool (such as Apache Bench) to simulate heavy traffic on your LoadBalancer Service.

- **Steps:**
  Monitor how the Service and autoscaling respond. Adjust resource limits if necessary.

- **Outcome:**
  Understand the practical implications of sudden load spikes and see autoscaling in action.

---

7. Final Thoughts and Encouragement

Exposing your applications and ensuring they remain accessible under varying loads is a critical aspect of modern application deployment. Kubernetes Services provide a powerful and flexible way to achieve this. By mastering Service Discovery and Load Balancing, you equip yourself with the tools necessary to build robust, scalable applications that can adapt to real-world demands.

It's natural to feel challenged when learning these concepts, but remember: every step you take—whether it's creating a simple NodePort Service or configuring autoscaling for a high-traffic application—builds your confidence and skill set. Use your local Kubernetes cluster as a playground. Experiment with different configurations, simulate real-world traffic, and tweak your settings to see what works best.

As you progress, keep the following in mind:

- Stay curious and ask questions when something isn't clear.

- Document your experiments, so you have a reference for future projects.

- Engage with the community through forums and discussion groups—chances are, someone else has faced the same challenges.

You have the foundation now to take on even more advanced topics, such as integrating service meshes, implementing advanced load balancing algorithms, and managing complex multi-region deployments. But for today, celebrate the progress you've made in understanding how Kubernetes makes your applications discoverable and resilient under load.

Remember, every expert was once a beginner. With persistence, practice, and a willingness to learn from mistakes, you will master these concepts. You can do this—one service, one deployment, one load spike at a time.

CHAPTER 6:
CONFIGURATION AND SECRETS MANAGEMENT

Welcome to this in-depth chapter on Configuration and Secrets Management in Kubernetes. In this chapter, we'll cover two critical aspects of managing applications in production: how to manage configuration data using ConfigMaps and how to store sensitive information safely with Secrets. We'll explore these concepts through everyday examples, clear explanations, and hands-on projects. You'll learn how to keep your application settings organized and secure, and you'll be guided through a project that demonstrates securing an application's configuration step by step.

Imagine you're running a busy café. You have recipes for your signature drinks that everyone in the kitchen follows, and some ingredients – like a secret blend of spices – are kept under lock and key. In the world of Kubernetes, ConfigMaps are like your recipes: they store non-sensitive configuration data that your application needs, while Secrets are like the locked vaults that store your secret

ingredients, ensuring that only those with the proper access can see them.

This chapter is designed to be friendly and approachable. We'll break down concepts into manageable pieces, use real-world analogies to make ideas relatable, and provide actionable steps that you can follow to secure your application configuration. Whether you're a beginner or a seasoned professional, you can take away practical tips and hands-on experience that are applicable in industries as varied as manufacturing, healthcare, and logistics.

---

1. Managing Configuration with ConfigMaps

1.1. What Are ConfigMaps?

In Kubernetes, a ConfigMap is a resource used to store configuration data in key-value pairs. Rather than hardcoding configuration values in your application code or container images, you can externalize them. This makes your applications more flexible, easier to update, and simpler to deploy across different environments.

Think of a ConfigMap as a digital bulletin board where you pin important notes, settings, and instructions that your application can read at runtime. For example, you might store URLs, feature flags, or environment-specific settings in a ConfigMap.

1.2. Why Use ConfigMaps?

Here are some reasons why ConfigMaps are so helpful:

- **Separation of Concerns:**
  By separating configuration from code, you can update settings without rebuilding your container images.

- **Environment Flexibility:**
  Use the same application image in development, testing, and production by simply changing the ConfigMap.

- **Centralized Management:**
  Manage configuration for multiple applications from a single

resource. This is especially useful when dealing with microservices.

Real-World Analogy

Imagine you're a chef who has written a set of recipes on a whiteboard in the kitchen. If you need to change an ingredient or adjust a cooking time, you simply update the whiteboard instead of rewriting the recipe book. In Kubernetes, the ConfigMap is that whiteboard, making it easy to update configuration details on the fly without touching your application code.

1.3. Creating a ConfigMap

Let's walk through a simple example of creating a ConfigMap. Suppose you have an application that needs a configuration file containing database connection details and API endpoints.

Step-by-Step Instructions

1. **Create a Configuration File:**

Create a file named app-config.properties with the following content:

properties

```
DATABASE_URL=postgres://user:password@db-host:5432/mydatabase
API_ENDPOINT=https://api.example.com/v1
FEATURE_FLAG=true
```

2. **Create the ConfigMap from the File:**

Use the following command to create a ConfigMap named app-config from the file:

bash

```
kubectl create configmap app-config --from-file=app-config.properties
```

This command tells Kubernetes to create a ConfigMap using the key-value pairs found in the file. Each line becomes a key and its corresponding value.

3. Verify the ConfigMap:

Check that your ConfigMap was created correctly by running:

bash

```
kubectl get configmaps app-config -o yaml
```
You should see the data from app-config.properties displayed in the output.

1.4. Using ConfigMaps in Pods

Once you have created a ConfigMap, you can use it in your Pods. There are several ways to incorporate a ConfigMap into a Pod:

- **As Environment Variables:**
  Map the key-value pairs from the ConfigMap into environment variables.

- **As Configuration Files:**
  Mount the ConfigMap as a volume so that the data appears as a file in the container's file system.

Example: Mounting a ConfigMap as a File

Let's modify a Pod's configuration to mount the app-config ConfigMap as a file.

1. Create a Pod YAML File:

Create a file named configmap-pod.yaml with the following content:

yaml

```
apiVersion: v1
kind: Pod
metadata:
  name: configmap-demo
  labels:
    app: configmap-demo
spec:
  containers:
  - name: demo-container
    image: busybox
    command: ["sh", "-c", "cat /etc/config/app-config.properties && sleep 3600"]
    volumeMounts:
    - name: config-volume
      mountPath: /etc/config
  volumes:
  - name: config-volume
    configMap:
      name: app-config
```

2. **Deploy the Pod:**

Run the command to deploy the Pod:

bash

kubectl apply -f configmap-pod.yaml

3. **Verify the Output:**

Once the Pod is running, check its logs:

bash

kubectl logs configmap-demo

You should see the contents of app-config.properties printed out.
This confirms that your Pod has successfully mounted the
ConfigMap as a file.

1.5. Updating a ConfigMap

One of the benefits of using ConfigMaps is that you can update configuration data without rebuilding your application. However, remember that changes to a ConfigMap don't automatically propagate to running Pods. You may need to restart or re-create Pods to pick up the new configuration.

How to Update a ConfigMap

1. **Edit the Configuration File:**

Open app-config.properties in your editor and change a value, such as updating the API endpoint:

properties

API_ENDPOINT=https://api.newexample.com/v2

2. **Update the ConfigMap:**

Re-create the ConfigMap by running:

bash

```
kubectl create configmap app-config --from-file=app-config.properties -o yaml --dry-run=client | kubectl apply -f -
```

3. **Restart Affected Pods:**

To apply the new configuration, restart the Pods that use the ConfigMap. For example:

bash

```
kubectl delete pod configmap-demo
```

Kubernetes will create a new Pod that mounts the updated ConfigMap.

2. Storing Sensitive Information Using Secrets

While ConfigMaps are great for storing non-sensitive configuration data, sensitive information – like passwords, API keys, or certificates – should be handled with extra care. Kubernetes provides a dedicated resource called a **Secret** to store such data in an encoded format.

2.1. What Are Secrets?

A Secret in Kubernetes is similar to a ConfigMap but is intended for storing confidential information. Data in Secrets is base64 encoded by default, offering a layer of protection against accidental exposure. However, it's important to note that base64 encoding is not encryption—it's merely an encoding scheme. For enhanced security, consider integrating additional encryption mechanisms when necessary.

Real-World Analogy

Imagine Secrets as the safe deposit boxes in a bank. While everyone might see the bank's exterior (the ConfigMaps that store general information), the safe deposit boxes hold your valuables, locked away and accessible only to those with the correct keys. In Kubernetes, Secrets store your sensitive data, ensuring that only authorized applications or users can access them.

2.2. Creating a Secret

Let's walk through creating a Secret to store some sensitive information, such as database credentials.

Step-by-Step Instructions

1. **Prepare the Sensitive Data:**

Create a file called db-creds.txt with the following content (this file contains a sample password):

plaintext

password=mysecretpassword

2. **Create the Secret from the File:**

Use the following command to create a Secret named db-secret:

bash

```
kubectl create secret generic db-secret --from-file=db-creds.txt
```

This command creates a Secret where the key is the filename (db-creds.txt) and the value is the content of the file, base64 encoded.

3. **Verify the Secret:**

Run the command to check the Secret:

bash

```
kubectl get secret db-secret -o yaml
```

You should see the key and the encoded value in the output.

2.3. Using Secrets in Pods

Similar to ConfigMaps, Secrets can be used in Pods either as environment variables or mounted as files.

Example: Mounting a Secret as a File

1. **Create a Pod YAML File:**

Create a file named secret-pod.yaml with the following content:

yaml

```
apiVersion: v1
kind: Pod
metadata:
  name: secret-demo
  labels:
    app: secret-demo
spec:
  containers:
  - name: demo-container
    image: busybox
    command: ["sh", "-c", "cat /etc/secret/db-creds.txt && sleep 3600"]
    volumeMounts:
    - name: secret-volume
      mountPath: /etc/secret
  volumes:
  - name: secret-volume
    secret:
      secretName: db-secret
```

2. Deploy the Pod:

Run the command to create the Pod:

bash

```
kubectl apply -f secret-pod.yaml
```

3. Verify the Output:

Check the logs of the Pod:

bash

```
kubectl logs secret-demo
```

You should see the content of db-creds.txt printed out (in this case, "password=mysecretpassword"). This confirms that the Secret has been successfully mounted.

2.4. Using Secrets as Environment Variables

Another way to use Secrets is to map them to environment variables in your Pod's container.

Example: Environment Variable Mapping

1. **Create a Pod YAML File:**

Create a file named secret-env-pod.yaml with the following content:

yaml

```
apiVersion: v1
kind: Pod
metadata:
  name: secret-env-demo
  labels:
    app: secret-env-demo
spec:
  containers:
  - name: demo-container
    image: busybox
    command: ["sh", "-c", "echo DB_PASSWORD=$DB_PASSWORD &&
sleep 3600"]
    env:
    - name: DB_PASSWORD
      valueFrom:
        secretKeyRef:
          name: db-secret
          key: db-creds.txt
```

2. **Deploy the Pod:**

Run:

bash

```
kubectl apply -f secret-env-pod.yaml
```

3. **Verify the Output:**

Check the logs:

```bash
```

kubectl logs secret-env-demo

The logs should display the environment variable DB_PASSWORD with the value stored in the Secret.

---

3. Project: Securing Your Application Configuration

In this project, you will combine the concepts of ConfigMaps and Secrets to secure your application configuration. Imagine you have a web application that requires both general configuration (non-sensitive) and sensitive data such as API keys and database credentials. Your task is to deploy this application in a way that externalizes its configuration using ConfigMaps and protects sensitive data using Secrets.

3.1. Project Overview

You will:

- Create a ConfigMap for non-sensitive configuration.

- Create a Secret for sensitive data.

- Deploy a sample web application that consumes both the ConfigMap and the Secret.

- Test the application to ensure that configuration values and secrets are accessible only where they should be.

Real-World Scenario

Picture a scenario in a healthcare facility where a patient management system requires general settings (like server endpoints and feature toggles) that can be updated on the fly, along with sensitive patient data that must remain secure. In our project, the ConfigMap holds the general settings, and the Secret keeps the sensitive data locked down.

3.2. Step 1: Prepare Your Configuration Files

1. General Configuration:

Create a file named app-settings.properties with the following content:

properties

```
APP_MODE=production
LOG_LEVEL=info
API_BASE_URL=https://api.healthcare-example.com
```

2. Sensitive Data:

Create a file named credentials.txt with the following content:

plaintext

```
dbUser=healthcare_admin
dbPassword=supersecret123
```

3.3. Step 2: Create the ConfigMap and Secret

1. Create the ConfigMap:

Run the following command to create a ConfigMap named app-config from app-settings.properties:

bash

```
kubectl create configmap app-config --from-file=app-settings.properties
```

2. Create the Secret:

Run this command to create a Secret named app-credentials from credentials.txt:

bash

```
kubectl create secret generic app-credentials --from-file=credentials.txt
```

3. Verify Both Resources:

Check the ConfigMap:

bash

```
kubectl get configmap app-config -o yaml
```

And check the Secret:

bash

```
kubectl get secret app-credentials -o yaml
```

3.4. Step 3: Deploy the Sample Application

Now, you will create a Deployment that uses both the ConfigMap and the Secret.

1. Create a Deployment YAML File:

Create a file named secured-app-deployment.yaml with the following content:

yaml

```
apiVersion: apps/v1
kind: Deployment
metadata:
  name: secured-app
  labels:
    app: secured-app
```

```
spec:
 replicas: 2
 selector:
  matchLabels:
   app: secured-app
 template:
  metadata:
   labels:
    app: secured-app
  spec:
   containers:
   - name: secured-container
     image: busybox
     command: ["sh", "-c", "echo 'App Mode: ' $(cat /etc/config/app-
settings.properties | grep APP_MODE) && echo 'DB User: ' $DB_USER &&
sleep 3600"]
     env:
     - name: DB_USER
       valueFrom:
        secretKeyRef:
         name: app-credentials
         key: credentials.txt
     volumeMounts:
     - name: config-volume
       mountPath: /etc/config
   volumes:
   - name: config-volume
     configMap:
      name: app-config
```

In this configuration:

o   The container reads general settings from the
    mounted ConfigMap.

o   The sensitive database user is provided as an
    environment variable from the Secret.

o   The command prints out values so you can verify that
    the data is being correctly accessed.

2. **Deploy the Application:**

Run:
bash

kubectl apply -f secured-app-deployment.yaml
3. **Verify the Deployment:**

Check that the Pods are running:

bash

kubectl get pods -l app=secured-app
4. **Review the Logs:**

Check the logs to verify the output:

bash

kubectl logs <pod-name>
You should see messages that include the app mode and database user details.

3.5. Step 4: Updating Configurations Securely

Once your application is running, you might need to update configurations or secrets. Here are some tips for safe handling and updates:

- **Version Control:**
  Keep all your YAML files in a version-controlled repository. This helps you track changes and revert if needed.

- **Immutable ConfigMaps and Secrets:**
  Consider creating new ConfigMaps or Secrets rather than updating existing ones. This practice helps avoid unintentional disruptions.

- **Rolling Updates:**
  When you update a ConfigMap or Secret, restart the Pods so they pick up the new changes.

- **Audit and Monitor:**
  Regularly check who has access to Secrets and monitor access logs if available.

---

4. Tips for Safe Handling and Updates

Here are some best practices to ensure that your configuration and secret management remains secure and efficient:

4.1. Least Privilege Principle

Always restrict access to Secrets and sensitive data. Ensure that only the applications and users that need access can view or modify these resources. This reduces the risk of accidental exposure.

4.2. Encryption in Transit and at Rest

While Kubernetes encodes Secret data in base64, consider enabling encryption at rest for Secrets in your cluster. Additionally, ensure that all communication between components is encrypted using TLS.

4.3. Regular Auditing

Periodically audit your ConfigMaps and Secrets. Remove any outdated or unused configurations, and review access permissions regularly. This helps you keep the configuration landscape clean and secure.

4.4. Automate Updates

Integrate your configuration and secret management into your CI/CD pipelines. Automating the deployment of updates minimizes manual errors and ensures that changes are applied consistently across environments.

4.5. Use External Secrets Management Solutions

For higher security requirements, consider integrating with external secrets management tools such as HashiCorp Vault, AWS Secrets Manager, or Azure Key Vault. These solutions offer advanced features like dynamic secrets, access logging, and fine-grained permission controls.

4.6. Document Everything

Maintain detailed documentation for your configuration and secret management strategies. Document what each ConfigMap and Secret is used for, how they are updated, and who has access. This documentation is invaluable when troubleshooting issues or onboarding new team members.

5. Recap and Key Takeaways

Let's summarize the key points covered in this chapter:

- **ConfigMaps:**

- Store non-sensitive configuration data as key-value pairs.

- Help externalize configuration from application code.

- Can be mounted as files or injected as environment variables.

- **Secrets:**

  - Store sensitive data such as passwords and API keys.

  - Provide a way to encode data, though additional encryption may be required.

  - Can be used similarly to ConfigMaps for injecting data into Pods.

- **Hands-On Project:**

  - We created a ConfigMap for general configuration and a Secret for sensitive data.

  - Deployed a sample application that uses both, verifying the integration by checking container logs.

- **Best Practices:**

  - Apply the least privilege principle, use encryption, audit regularly, automate updates, and consider external secrets management solutions.

  - Document all configurations and changes for security and troubleshooting.

6. Additional Exercises and Challenges

To deepen your understanding, here are some exercises you can try on your own:

Exercise 1: Create Multiple ConfigMaps

- **Task:**
  Create separate ConfigMaps for different application modules (e.g., one for logging settings, one for API endpoints).

- **Steps:**
  Write YAML files for each ConfigMap, apply them, and then create a multi-container Pod that mounts each ConfigMap in different directories.

- **Outcome:**
  Gain experience in organizing configuration data for complex applications.

Exercise 2: Rotate Secrets Regularly

- **Task:**
  Simulate a secret rotation process where you update a Secret with new values.

- **Steps:**
  Create an initial Secret, deploy a Pod that uses it, then update the Secret with new data and restart the Pod.

- **Outcome:**
  Learn how to manage and automate secret rotation without downtime.

Exercise 3: Integrate with an External Secrets Manager

- **Task:**
  Explore integration with an external secrets management tool (for example, HashiCorp Vault).

- **Steps:**
  Follow a tutorial to configure Vault, store a secret, and then use a Kubernetes Secret Store CSI driver to inject the secret into a Pod.

- **Outcome:**
  Understand advanced security techniques and how they can be combined with Kubernetes native features.

Exercise 4: Audit and Monitor Configuration Changes

- **Task:**
  Set up a process for monitoring changes to ConfigMaps and Secrets.

- **Steps:**
  Use Kubernetes audit logs or a third-party monitoring tool to track changes.

- **Outcome:**
  Build a habit of regular auditing to catch misconfigurations early.

---

7. Final Thoughts and Encouragement

Managing configuration and secrets effectively is a cornerstone of running secure and resilient applications. By separating non-sensitive settings from sensitive data, you gain the flexibility to update configurations without modifying your code and protect critical information from unauthorized access.

Remember, the process of setting up ConfigMaps and Secrets might seem overwhelming at first, but each step you take builds your expertise. Whether you're managing configurations for a small application or a complex microservices architecture, these techniques scale with you. Your local Kubernetes cluster is a safe space to experiment and refine your configuration management skills.

Take pride in the hands-on project you've completed in this chapter. You've learned how to externalize your application's settings, secure sensitive data, and handle updates in a controlled manner. These skills are directly applicable in many real-world scenarios—whether you're working in healthcare, manufacturing, or logistics, the ability to manage configurations and secrets securely is invaluable.

As you continue on your Kubernetes journey, keep experimenting with new configurations, automate your update processes, and document everything. Each new challenge is an opportunity to learn and improve. Always remember that every expert started exactly where you are now—by taking it one step at a time.

You've got the tools, you've learned the techniques, and now it's time to apply them. Trust in your ability to secure and manage your application configurations, and know that with persistence and practice, you will master these concepts.

Happy coding, and here's to building secure, scalable applications—one ConfigMap and Secret at a time!

CHAPTER 7:
PERSISTENT STORAGE
IN KUBERNETES

Welcome to this comprehensive chapter on Persistent Storage in Kubernetes. In modern application deployments, managing persistent data is just as important as running containers. Whether you're dealing with databases, logs, or any stateful application data, Kubernetes offers powerful tools to help you manage storage effectively. This chapter will walk you through the essentials of persistent storage in Kubernetes, including an overview of volumes, persistent volumes (PVs), and persistent volume claims (PVCs). We'll then guide you through a hands-on project integrating a database with persistent storage, and finally, discuss strategies for managing stateful applications in real-world scenarios.

Imagine running a bakery where fresh ingredients are delivered daily, and you need to store recipes, inventory, and customer orders securely and reliably. Containers are like the ovens and mixers that produce your baked goods – efficient and disposable – but the recipes and orders must be preserved. In Kubernetes, persistent storage is the pantry and filing cabinet that holds your critical data even when the production equipment is restarted or replaced.

Throughout this chapter, we'll use relatable analogies, clear explanations, and actionable projects to help you understand and implement persistent storage in your Kubernetes environment. Whether you're working in manufacturing, healthcare, logistics, or any industry that relies on reliable data storage, you can follow along with confidence. Let's get started!

1. Overview of Volumes and Persistent Storage

1.1. Understanding Kubernetes Volumes

In Kubernetes, a volume is a directory accessible to the containers in a Pod. Unlike traditional container storage, Kubernetes volumes outlive the life of a container. This means that if a container crashes or is restarted, the data in the volume remains available. Volumes come in many types, ranging from emptyDir (ephemeral) to more durable options like hostPath, NFS, or cloud provider-specific volumes.

Imagine a volume as a reusable notebook in a classroom. Even if one student (container) leaves or restarts their work, the notes (data) in the notebook remain available for the next session. This continuity is essential for applications that require data persistence across container restarts.

1.2. The Need for Persistent Storage

While volumes are great for sharing data among containers in a Pod, many applications require storage that persists beyond the life of a Pod. For example, databases, log aggregators, or content management systems need to store data that must survive Pod restarts and even Pod rescheduling across nodes. Persistent storage ensures that data remains intact and available regardless of the transient nature of Pods.

Think of persistent storage as a safe deposit box. Even if the vault (Pod) is moved or replaced, the safe deposit box remains intact with all your valuables inside.

1.3. Persistent Volumes (PVs)

A Persistent Volume (PV) is a piece of storage in the cluster that has been provisioned by an administrator or dynamically provisioned using Storage Classes. PVs are resources in the cluster just like nodes are resources. They have a lifecycle independent of any individual Pod that uses the PV.

Key Characteristics of PVs:

- **Decoupled from Pods:**
  PVs exist independently, allowing you to reuse them across multiple Pods and deployments.

- **Pre-provisioned or Dynamic:**
  Storage can be manually provisioned by administrators or automatically created using dynamic provisioning.

- **Defined by Storage Classes:**
  Storage Classes define different tiers or types of storage, such as SSDs versus HDDs, or high-availability versus standard performance.

1.4. Persistent Volume Claims (PVCs)

A Persistent Volume Claim (PVC) is a request for storage by a user. It specifies size, access modes (e.g., ReadWriteOnce, ReadOnlyMany, or ReadWriteMany), and other storage requirements. When a PVC is created, Kubernetes looks for a matching PV. If it finds one that meets the criteria, the PVC is bound to that PV.

Imagine a PVC as a reservation request at a storage facility. You specify how much space you need and any special requirements, and if a matching storage unit (PV) is available, you can start using it.

1.5. How PVs and PVCs Work Together

The PV-PVC relationship is a powerful abstraction in Kubernetes. It decouples storage management from application management, allowing developers to request storage without worrying about the underlying details.

- **Binding Process:**
  When a PVC is created, Kubernetes' control plane finds a suitable PV that satisfies the claim's requirements. Once found, the PVC is bound to that PV.

- **Reusability:**
  After a Pod using a PVC is terminated, the PV can be reused by another Pod, ensuring that your data persists and remains accessible.

- **Dynamic Provisioning:**
  If no existing PV matches the claim, Kubernetes can dynamically provision a new PV based on a Storage Class, making it easier to scale and manage storage needs.

2. Setting Up Persistent Volumes and Claims

In this section, we'll walk through the process of setting up persistent storage in Kubernetes. We will cover both pre-provisioned and dynamically provisioned storage using PVs and PVCs.

2.1. Pre-provisioned Persistent Volumes

In some cases, an administrator might manually create a PV that represents storage available in the cluster. This process is common in on-premise environments where storage is managed separately from the cluster.

Step-by-Step Example of a Pre-provisioned PV

1. **Create a PV YAML File:**

Create a file called pv.yaml with the following content:

```yaml
apiVersion: v1
kind: PersistentVolume
metadata:
  name: pv-demo
spec:
  capacity:
    storage: 1Gi
  accessModes:
    - ReadWriteOnce
  persistentVolumeReclaimPolicy: Retain
  hostPath:
    path: /mnt/data
```

This configuration creates a PV named pv-demo with a capacity of 1Gi, using the host's file system at /mnt/data.

2. **Deploy the PV:**

Apply the YAML file:

```bash
kubectl apply -f pv.yaml
```

3. **Verify the PV:**

Check the status with:

```bash
bash
```

```
kubectl get pv pv-demo
```

You should see that the PV is available and ready to be claimed.

2.2. Persistent Volume Claims (PVCs)

Now that we have a PV, we can create a PVC to claim that storage.

1. **Create a PVC YAML File:**

Create a file named pvc.yaml with the following content:

```yaml
yaml
```

```yaml
apiVersion: v1
kind: PersistentVolumeClaim
metadata:
  name: pvc-demo
spec:
  accessModes:
    - ReadWriteOnce
  resources:
    requests:
      storage: 500Mi
```

This PVC requests 500Mi of storage with ReadWriteOnce access.

2. **Deploy the PVC:**

Apply the PVC configuration:

```bash
bash
```

```
kubectl apply -f pvc.yaml
```

3. **Verify the Binding:**

Check that the PVC is bound to the PV:

```bash
bash
```

```
kubectl get pvc pvc-demo
```

The output should show that the PVC is bound to a PV (likely pv-demo if it matches the claim's requirements).

2.3. Dynamic Provisioning Using Storage Classes

Dynamic provisioning simplifies storage management by automatically creating PVs as needed. This method is common in cloud environments where storage classes abstract away the underlying storage infrastructure.

1. **Create a Storage Class YAML File:**

Create a file named storage-class.yaml with the following content (this example is for a generic provisioner; in cloud environments, you might specify a cloud provider's storage class):

yaml

```
apiVersion: storage.k8s.io/v1
kind: StorageClass
metadata:
  name: standard
provisioner: kubernetes.io/no-provisioner
volumeBindingMode: WaitForFirstConsumer
```

In production, replace kubernetes.io/no-provisioner with the appropriate provisioner for your environment (for example, kubernetes.io/aws-ebs for AWS).

2. **Deploy the Storage Class:**

Apply the YAML file:

bash

```
kubectl apply -f storage-class.yaml
```

3. **Create a PVC That Uses the Storage Class:**

Create a file called pvc-dynamic.yaml:

yaml

```
apiVersion: v1
kind: PersistentVolumeClaim
metadata:
  name: pvc-dynamic
spec:
  storageClassName: standard
  accessModes:
   - ReadWriteOnce
  resources:
   requests:
    storage: 1Gi
```
Deploy the PVC:
bash

```
kubectl apply -f pvc-dynamic.yaml
```
   4. **Verify the Dynamic PV Creation:**

After applying the PVC, Kubernetes should automatically create a PV based on the Storage Class. Verify with:

bash

```
kubectl get pv
kubectl get pvc pvc-dynamic
```
You'll see that a new PV has been dynamically provisioned and bound to pvc-dynamic.

---

3. Hands-on Project: Integrating a Database with Persistent Storage

To put these concepts into practice, let's work through a hands-on project where we integrate a database with persistent storage. In this project, you will deploy a database (using MySQL as an example) and ensure that its data is stored persistently, even if the Pod restarts.

3.1. Project Overview

You will:

- Create a PVC for persistent storage.

- Deploy a MySQL database using a Deployment.

- Mount the PVC in the MySQL container.

- Verify that the database retains data even if the Pod is restarted.

- Discuss considerations for managing stateful applications.

Imagine this project as setting up a secure filing system for a business. The database is your filing cabinet that holds all important records. The PVC ensures that, even if the database server (the Pod) is replaced, the records (data) remain safe and accessible.

3.2. Step 1: Creating a Persistent Volume Claim for MySQL

1. **Create a PVC YAML File:**

Create a file called mysql-pvc.yaml with the following content:

yaml

```
apiVersion: v1
kind: PersistentVolumeClaim
metadata:
  name: mysql-pvc
spec:
```

```
accessModes:
 - ReadWriteOnce
resources:
 requests:
   storage: 2Gi
```
This PVC requests 2Gi of storage for our MySQL database.

2. Deploy the PVC:

Run the command:

```bash
kubectl apply -f mysql-pvc.yaml
```

3. Verify the PVC:

Check the PVC status with:

```bash
kubectl get pvc mysql-pvc
```
Ensure that it is bound to a PV.

3.3. Step 2: Deploying MySQL with Persistent Storage

1. Create a MySQL Deployment YAML File:

Create a file called mysql-deployment.yaml with the following content:

```yaml
apiVersion: apps/v1
kind: Deployment
metadata:
 name: mysql-deployment
 labels:
   app: mysql
spec:
 replicas: 1
```

```
selector:
  matchLabels:
    app: mysql
template:
  metadata:
    labels:
      app: mysql
  spec:
    containers:
    - name: mysql
      image: mysql:5.7
      env:
      - name: MYSQL_ROOT_PASSWORD
        value: "my-secret-pw"
      - name: MYSQL_DATABASE
        value: "exampledb"
      ports:
      - containerPort: 3306
      volumeMounts:
      - name: mysql-storage
        mountPath: /var/lib/mysql
    volumes:
    - name: mysql-storage
      persistentVolumeClaim:
        claimName: mysql-pvc
```

This configuration deploys a MySQL container with the root password and an example database, mounting the PVC at /var/lib/mysql (the default data directory for MySQL).

2. **Deploy MySQL:**

Apply the YAML file:

bash

```
kubectl apply -f mysql-deployment.yaml
```

3. **Verify the Deployment:**

Check that the MySQL Pod is running:

bash

```
kubectl get pods -l app=mysql
```

3.4. Step 3: Testing Data Persistence

To confirm that your MySQL data is persistent, follow these steps:

1. Connect to the MySQL Pod:

Open a shell in the MySQL Pod:

bash

```
kubectl exec -it <mysql-pod-name> -- bash
```
Replace <mysql-pod-name> with the name of your running MySQL Pod.

2. Log into MySQL:

Once inside the Pod, log into the MySQL client:

bash

```
mysql -u root -p
```
Enter the password (my-secret-pw) when prompted.

3. Create a Test Table and Insert Data:

Run the following SQL commands:

sql

```
USE exampledb;
CREATE TABLE test (id INT AUTO_INCREMENT PRIMARY KEY,
message VARCHAR(255));
INSERT INTO test (message) VALUES ('Hello, Kubernetes!');
SELECT * FROM test;
```
Verify that the row is inserted correctly.

4. Exit and Restart the Pod:

Exit the MySQL client and then exit the Pod's shell. Now, delete the MySQL Pod to simulate a restart:

bash

```
kubectl delete pod <mysql-pod-name>
```

Kubernetes will automatically create a new Pod based on the Deployment.

5. **Verify Data Persistence:**

Once the new Pod is running, repeat steps 1–3. When you select from the test table, you should still see the previously inserted data. This confirms that the persistent storage is working as expected.

3.5. Step 4: Discussion on Managing Stateful Applications

Managing stateful applications, like databases, in a containerized environment introduces unique challenges compared to stateless applications. Here are some key considerations:

Data Integrity and Backup

- **Backups:**
  Always implement a backup strategy for critical data. This may involve periodic snapshots of persistent volumes or using database-specific backup tools.

- **Consistency:**
  Ensure that data is consistent during updates and rollouts. Some applications require special handling (like quiescing the database) before updates are applied.

Performance Considerations

- **Storage Performance:**
  The underlying storage technology can impact performance.

For high-performance applications, consider using SSD-based volumes or cloud provider options with high IOPS.

- **I/O Throughput:**
  Monitor the I/O throughput of your persistent volumes. High disk usage may require scaling or provisioning additional resources.

StatefulSets vs. Deployments

While we used a Deployment for our MySQL example, Kubernetes offers StatefulSets for managing stateful applications. StatefulSets provide guarantees about the ordering and uniqueness of Pods, making them ideal for applications that require stable network identities and persistent storage.

- **Stable Identifiers:**
  StatefulSets assign each Pod a unique, stable network identifier.

- **Ordered Deployment and Scaling:**
  Pods in a StatefulSet are created and scaled in a specific order, which is important for applications that require initialization in a particular sequence.

Real-World Analogy: The Library Archive

Consider a stateful application like a library archive. Books (data) must be preserved carefully, with records indicating their location and status. Unlike a pop-up bookstore (stateless applications) that can change its setup frequently, a library requires a robust system to ensure that every book is catalogued and accessible over time. In Kubernetes, StatefulSets provide the mechanisms needed to manage such archival systems, ensuring that data remains reliable and consistent.

4. Best Practices for Persistent Storage in Kubernetes

As you work with persistent storage in Kubernetes, keep the following best practices in mind to ensure that your applications remain reliable and your data secure:

4.1. Choose the Right Storage Class

- **Understand Your Needs:**
  Evaluate the performance, cost, and durability requirements of your application. Use a Storage Class that matches your workload.

- **Cloud vs. On-Premise:**
  In cloud environments, take advantage of managed storage solutions that offer high availability and scalability. For on-premise deployments, consider using NFS or local SSDs for performance.

4.2. Monitor Storage Usage

- **Metrics and Alerts:**
  Set up monitoring to track storage usage and performance. Tools like Prometheus and Grafana can help visualize metrics and alert you to potential issues.

- **Regular Audits:**
  Periodically review persistent volume usage and reclaim unused resources to avoid wasted capacity.

4.3. Backup and Recovery

- **Automate Backups:**
  Schedule regular backups of critical data stored in persistent volumes. Ensure that backups are stored securely and can be restored quickly.

- **Test Recovery Processes:**
  Regularly test your backup and recovery procedures to ensure that you can restore data in the event of a failure.

4.4. Use StatefulSets for Complex Stateful Applications

- **Evaluate the Workload:**
  For applications like databases, message queues, or distributed caches, consider using StatefulSets for better management of network identities and storage.

- **Plan for Data Migration:**
  When transitioning from Deployments to StatefulSets, plan carefully to migrate data without downtime.

4.5. Security and Access Control

- **Restrict Access:**
  Ensure that persistent volumes and the underlying storage are secured. Use Kubernetes RBAC and network policies to control access.

- **Encryption:**
  When possible, encrypt data at rest and in transit to protect sensitive information.

5. Recap and Key Takeaways

Let's review the key points covered in this chapter:

- **Volumes and Persistent Storage:**
  Kubernetes volumes provide a way to share data between containers, but persistent storage is required for stateful applications. Persistent Volumes (PVs) and Persistent Volume Claims (PVCs) decouple storage management from Pod lifecycles.

- **Setting Up Storage:**
  We covered both pre-provisioned storage and dynamic provisioning using Storage Classes. You learned how to create a PV, bind it with a PVC, and verify that it's working.

- **Hands-on Project – Integrating a Database:**
  Through a step-by-step project, you deployed a MySQL database with persistent storage. You tested data persistence by inserting data, restarting the Pod, and confirming that the data remained intact.

- **Managing Stateful Applications:**
  We discussed the challenges of running stateful applications in a containerized environment and introduced concepts like StatefulSets, backups, and performance monitoring.

- **Best Practices:**
  Choosing the right storage class, monitoring usage, automating backups, and securing your storage are critical for building reliable, scalable systems.

6. Additional Exercises and Challenges

To further reinforce your understanding and skills, try these additional exercises:

Exercise 1: Expand the Database Deployment

- **Task:**
  Add a read replica to your MySQL deployment using a StatefulSet.

- **Steps:**
  Create a StatefulSet configuration for the MySQL replicas, configure headless services for stable network identities, and test data replication between the primary and replica.

- **Outcome:**
  Understand how to scale a stateful database using Kubernetes and observe replication behavior.

Exercise 2: Implement a Backup Solution

- **Task:**
  Integrate a simple backup script into your MySQL deployment.

- **Steps:**
  Write a script that runs inside a sidecar container to periodically back up the MySQL data to an external storage location. Configure a CronJob in Kubernetes to automate the backup process.

- **Outcome:**
  Learn how to ensure data durability and recovery in case of failure.

Exercise 3: Performance Tuning

- **Task:**
  Simulate a high-load scenario on your MySQL database and monitor the performance of your persistent storage.

- **Steps:**
  Use a load testing tool to generate traffic, monitor disk I/O, and adjust resource requests and limits in your Deployment configuration.

- **Outcome:**
  Gain insights into how persistent storage performance impacts stateful applications under load.

Exercise 4: Explore Different Storage Backends

- **Task:**
  Experiment with different Storage Classes by using various storage backends (e.g., local SSDs, NFS, cloud provider volumes).

- **Steps:**
  Create multiple PVCs using different Storage Classes, deploy a test application that writes data to each, and compare performance and ease of management.

- **Outcome:**
  Develop an understanding of how different storage solutions affect application performance and reliability.

---

7. Final Thoughts and Encouragement

Persistent storage is a critical piece of the puzzle when it comes to running real-world applications on Kubernetes. While containers are ephemeral, data is not. Your ability to configure and manage persistent storage effectively can make the difference between an application that loses its state on every restart and one that reliably serves its users, even under challenging conditions.

Throughout this chapter, we've walked through the concepts, provided step-by-step projects, and discussed best practices to give you a robust foundation in persistent storage. As you continue your Kubernetes journey, remember:

- **Take It One Step at a Time:**
  Learning persistent storage management might seem daunting at first. Start with simple setups, test thoroughly, and gradually build up to more complex scenarios.

- **Experiment and Learn:**
  Your local Kubernetes cluster is your sandbox. Try out different configurations, simulate failures, and observe how your applications respond.

- **Document Your Work:**
  Keeping detailed notes of your configuration files, changes, and observations will not only help you troubleshoot but also build a reference library for future projects.

- **Stay Curious:**
  The world of persistent storage is evolving, with new storage solutions and best practices emerging regularly. Engage with the community, read updated documentation, and continuously refine your approach.

- **You Can Do It:**
  Every expert was once a beginner. With practice and persistence, you'll master the art of managing persistent storage in Kubernetes.

As you integrate these practices into your projects—whether you're deploying a critical database for a healthcare application or a logging system for a manufacturing plant—you'll find that robust, persistent storage is the backbone of a reliable, scalable system.

Take a deep breath, trust in your growing skills, and remember that every challenge you overcome is a step toward becoming a Kubernetes pro. Happy coding, and here's to building applications that keep your data safe, sound, and always available!

CHAPTER 8: MONITORING, LOGGING, AND TROUBLESHOOTING

Welcome to this comprehensive chapter on Monitoring, Logging, and Troubleshooting in Kubernetes. When you run applications in a distributed environment, it's essential to keep an eye on how everything is performing, quickly detect problems, and diagnose issues when they occur. This chapter will guide you through the tools and strategies you need to monitor your clusters, set up logging and alerts, and troubleshoot issues effectively.

Imagine you're running a fleet of delivery trucks. You want to know where each truck is at all times, whether it's running efficiently, and if there's any breakdown, you need a system in place that alerts you instantly so that repairs can be made before the problem affects your entire operation. Monitoring, logging, and troubleshooting in Kubernetes serve that same purpose for your applications and infrastructure.

In this chapter, we'll break down complex concepts into easy-to-understand segments, use relatable analogies to illustrate the ideas, and provide you with a hands-on project where you will build a monitoring dashboard. Whether you work in manufacturing, healthcare, logistics, or any industry that depends on reliable application performance, the techniques and tools covered here will help you stay on top of your systems. Let's dive in!

1. Tools and Strategies for Monitoring Clusters

1.1. Why Monitoring Is Essential

Monitoring is the process of continuously checking the health, performance, and resource usage of your Kubernetes clusters. It helps you ensure that your applications are running as expected, provides insights into system behavior, and alerts you to potential issues before they escalate.

Imagine a restaurant where the chef not only prepares meals but also keeps an eye on every dish that leaves the kitchen. If something seems off—perhaps a dish is taking too long or ingredients are running low—the chef intervenes to fix the problem. Similarly, monitoring in Kubernetes lets you intervene before a small hiccup becomes a full-blown crisis.

1.2. Key Metrics to Monitor

When setting up monitoring for a Kubernetes cluster, it's important to focus on key metrics that give you insights into overall health and performance:

- **Cluster Health:**
  Monitor the status of nodes and Pods. Are all nodes running? Are there any failed Pods?

- **Resource Usage:**
  Track CPU, memory, and storage usage on both nodes and Pods. This helps prevent resource exhaustion.

- **Network Traffic:**
  Monitor network latency, packet loss, and bandwidth usage

to ensure that communication between components is efficient.

- **Application Performance:**
  Look at response times, error rates, and throughput of your applications to spot performance bottlenecks.

- **Custom Metrics:**
  Depending on your application, you might need to monitor specific metrics like the number of active users, order rates, or sensor data in an industrial environment.

1.3. Popular Monitoring Tools

There are several tools available for monitoring Kubernetes clusters. Here are a few widely adopted ones:

- **Prometheus:**
  An open-source monitoring and alerting toolkit designed for reliability and scalability. It collects and stores metrics in a time-series database and supports powerful querying via PromQL.

- **Grafana:**
  A tool for visualizing metrics collected by Prometheus or other data sources. Grafana dashboards help you create interactive graphs and alerts.

- **Kube-state-metrics:**
  A service that listens to the Kubernetes API server and generates metrics about the state of objects, such as deployments and pods.

- **cAdvisor:**
  Provides container resource usage and performance

characteristics, integrated into the kubelet, giving you detailed insights into container-level metrics.

- **ELK/EFK Stack (Elasticsearch, Logstash/Fluentd, Kibana):** For logging, these tools allow you to collect, store, and analyze log data from your Kubernetes clusters.

1.4. Strategies for Effective Monitoring

Setting up a monitoring system isn't just about installing tools; it's about implementing strategies that ensure you catch issues early and respond appropriately.

Strategy 1: Establish Baselines

Before you can detect anomalies, you need to know what normal behavior looks like. Monitor your clusters over time to establish performance baselines. This helps you set thresholds for alerts.

Strategy 2: Alerting

Configure alerts to notify you when metrics exceed certain thresholds. Alerts can be sent via email, SMS, or integrated messaging platforms like Slack. Timely alerts are essential to quickly address issues.

Strategy 3: Use Dashboards

Create intuitive dashboards that display the most critical metrics in real time. Visual representations of data help you quickly grasp the state of your cluster and spot trends.

Strategy 4: Log Aggregation

Centralize your logs from all components. Aggregated logs make it easier to search for issues and correlate events across multiple services.

Strategy 5: Automate Responses

Where possible, automate remediation for common issues. For instance, auto-scaling policies or restarting failing Pods can help maintain stability without manual intervention.

---

2. Setting Up Logging and Alerts

2.1. Importance of Logging

Logs are a goldmine of information when it comes to understanding what's happening inside your applications and the cluster. They capture events, errors, and other important messages that can help you diagnose issues after the fact.

Think of logs as the black boxes in airplanes. They record every detail, which can be invaluable when something goes wrong. Without logs, troubleshooting can become guesswork.

2.2. Log Collection Strategies

Collecting logs efficiently requires the right architecture. In Kubernetes, you have a few common approaches:

- **Sidecar Containers:**
  Deploy a sidecar container in your Pod that handles log collection and shipping to a central repository.

- **DaemonSets:**
  Use a DaemonSet to run a log collector on every node in the cluster. Tools like Fluentd or Filebeat are popular choices.

- **Centralized Logging Systems:**
  Implement a centralized logging system using the ELK (Elasticsearch, Logstash, Kibana) or EFK (Elasticsearch, Fluentd, Kibana) stack. This system aggregates logs from all Pods and nodes, providing a unified view for analysis.

2.3. Setting Up Alerts

Alerts are essential for proactive monitoring. When a metric goes out of the acceptable range, an alert informs you so that you can take action before the problem escalates.

Steps to Set Up Alerts with Prometheus and Grafana:

1. **Install Prometheus:**
   Deploy Prometheus in your cluster. There are many Helm charts available to simplify the process.

2. **Define Alert Rules:**
   Create alert rules in Prometheus. For example, you might set an alert for high CPU usage:

yaml

```
groups:
- name: cluster-alerts
  rules:
  - alert: HighCPUUsage
    expr: sum(rate(container_cpu_usage_seconds_total[2m])) by (pod) > 0.8
    for: 2m
    labels:
      severity: warning
    annotations:
      summary: "High CPU usage detected for pod {{ $labels.pod }}"
```

description: "CPU usage is above 80% for more than 2 minutes."

3. **Integrate with Alertmanager:**
   Configure Alertmanager to send alerts to your preferred communication channels (email, Slack, etc.).

4. **Visualize Alerts in Grafana:**
   Use Grafana dashboards to display alerts alongside performance metrics for context.

2.4. Log Retention and Analysis

Decide how long you need to keep your logs and set up retention policies accordingly. Storage costs and regulatory requirements can influence these decisions. Once logs are stored centrally, you can use tools like Kibana to analyze patterns, search for error messages, and correlate logs with events.

3. Hands-on Project: Implementing a Monitoring Dashboard

In this project, you'll implement a monitoring dashboard using Prometheus and Grafana. This dashboard will help you visualize key metrics from your Kubernetes cluster, set up alerts, and provide a central location for troubleshooting.

3.1. Project Overview

You will:

- Deploy Prometheus in your Kubernetes cluster.

- Deploy Grafana and configure it to use Prometheus as a data source.

- Create dashboards to visualize metrics such as CPU usage, memory usage, and Pod status.

- Set up a simple alert rule and verify that alerts are triggered when conditions are met.

Imagine this project as setting up a control room for a power plant. The control room displays real-time data from all parts of the facility, and operators can quickly identify and respond to issues.

3.2. Step 1: Deploying Prometheus

Using Helm to Install Prometheus

Helm makes it easier to deploy applications in Kubernetes. First, ensure you have Helm installed and configured.

1. **Add the Prometheus Helm Repository:**

bash

```
helm repo add prometheus-community https://prometheus-community.github.io/helm-charts
helm repo update
```

2. **Install Prometheus:** Deploy Prometheus using the Helm chart:

bash

```
helm install prometheus prometheus-community/prometheus
```
This command deploys Prometheus and all its components (server, node exporters, etc.) in your cluster.

3. **Verify the Deployment:** Check the status of the Prometheus Pods:

```bash
kubectl get pods -l "app=prometheus"
```
Ensure that the Prometheus server and other components are running.

3.3. Step 2: Deploying Grafana

1. **Add the Grafana Helm Repository (if not already added):**

```bash
helm repo add grafana https://grafana.github.io/helm-charts
helm repo update
```

2. **Install Grafana:** Use Helm to deploy Grafana:

```bash
helm install grafana grafana/grafana
```
This command deploys Grafana, which includes a default dashboard and configuration options.

3. **Access Grafana:** Once Grafana is deployed, expose it using a NodePort or port-forward:

```bash
kubectl port-forward service/grafana 3000:80
```
Open your browser and navigate to http://localhost:3000. Log in using the default credentials (username: admin, password: admin – you may be prompted to change the password).

3.4. Step 3: Configuring Grafana to Use Prometheus

1. **Add Prometheus as a Data Source in Grafana:**

   o In Grafana, click on **Configuration** (the gear icon) and select **Data Sources**.

- ○ Click **Add data source**, then select **Prometheus**.

- ○ Set the URL to point to your Prometheus server. If Prometheus is running in the same cluster and exposed via a service, you might set the URL to something like http://prometheus-server.

- ○ Click **Save & Test** to ensure Grafana can connect to Prometheus.

2. **Import or Create Dashboards:**

- ○ You can import pre-built dashboards from the Grafana dashboard repository or create your own.

- ○ For a custom dashboard, add panels for metrics such as:

  - **CPU Usage:** Use a query like sum(rate(container_cpu_usage_seconds_total[1m])) by (pod)

  - **Memory Usage:** Use a query like sum(container_memory_usage_bytes) by (pod)

  - **Node Status:** Display node health and resource utilization.

3.5. Step 4: Setting Up an Alert

1. **Create a Simple Alert Rule in Prometheus:** Edit the Prometheus alert rules configuration (this might be part of the Helm chart's values file). For example:

yaml

```
groups:
- name: kubernetes-alerts
  rules:
  - alert: HighMemoryUsage
    expr: sum(container_memory_usage_bytes) by (pod) > 500000000
    for: 3m
    labels:
      severity: warning
    annotations:
      summary: "High memory usage detected on pod {{ $labels.pod }}"
      description: "Memory usage has exceeded 500MB for more than 3
minutes."
```

Deploy or update the alert rules accordingly.

2. **Test the Alert:** To simulate high memory usage, you can
   create a load test or temporarily modify the threshold. Once
   the conditions are met, check Alertmanager (or your alerting
   integration) to see if the alert is triggered.

3.6. Step 5: Verifying and Troubleshooting the Dashboard

1. **Interact with the Dashboard:** Use Grafana to interact with
   your dashboards. Verify that data is flowing from
   Prometheus, and adjust panel queries as needed to capture
   the most important metrics.

2. **Troubleshooting Common Issues:**

   o **No Data Displayed:**
      Check that the Prometheus data source URL is
      correct and that Prometheus is collecting metrics.

   o **Alerts Not Triggering:**
      Ensure that the alert rules in Prometheus are

correctly configured and that the metrics exceed the defined thresholds.

- ○ **Grafana Access Issues:**
  If you can't access Grafana, verify that port-forwarding or NodePort settings are correctly configured.

By the end of this project, you'll have a functional monitoring dashboard that not only displays critical metrics from your Kubernetes cluster but also alerts you to potential issues. This hands-on experience will give you the confidence to manage and troubleshoot your clusters effectively.

---

4. Approaches for Diagnosing and Resolving Issues

Even with the best monitoring and logging in place, issues will occur. Diagnosing and resolving these issues quickly is critical to maintaining a healthy, performant cluster.

4.1. Common Issues in Kubernetes

Some typical issues you might encounter include:

- **Resource Exhaustion:**
  Pods or nodes running out of CPU, memory, or storage.

- **Network Latency and Connectivity Problems:**
  Communication issues between Pods or with external services.

- **Application Errors:**
  Misconfigurations or bugs that lead to application crashes.

- **Deployment Failures:**
  Issues with rolling updates or Pod scheduling.

4.2. Tools for Diagnosis

When issues arise, the following tools and commands are invaluable:

- **kubectl:**
  Use commands like kubectl get pods, kubectl describe pod <pod-name>, and kubectl logs <pod-name> to inspect the state and logs of your resources.

- **Prometheus and Grafana:**
  Use your dashboards to spot anomalies in resource usage, latency, and error rates.

- **ELK/EFK Stack:**
  Centralized logging systems that let you search logs across multiple containers and nodes.

- **Debugging Tools:**
  Tools like kubectl exec allow you to run commands in a running Pod for real-time troubleshooting.

4.3. Troubleshooting Strategies

Strategy 1: Isolate the Problem

When an issue occurs, try to narrow down the scope:

- **Check Logs:**
  Look at the logs of the affected Pods to see if there are error messages or unusual behavior.

- **Verify Metrics:**
  Use your monitoring dashboard to check if resource usage spikes correlate with the issue.

- **Test Connectivity:**
  If the problem seems network-related, test connectivity between Pods using commands like curl or ping.

Strategy 2: Incremental Diagnosis

Start with high-level cluster health, then drill down:

- **Cluster Overview:**
  Run kubectl get nodes and kubectl get pods to ensure that all components are running.

- **Pod-Level Checks:**
  Identify any Pods in a CrashLoopBackOff or Error state. Use kubectl describe to get more details.

- **Container Logs:**
  Use kubectl logs to inspect logs for errors or warnings.

- **Review Recent Changes:**
  Consider what has changed recently in your configuration or deployment that might have triggered the issue.

Strategy 3: Rollbacks and Redeployments

If an update causes issues:

- **Roll Back:**
  Use kubectl rollout undo for Deployments to revert to a previous stable state.

- **Redeploy:**
  Sometimes, simply redeploying a Pod or Deployment can resolve transient issues.

4.4. Real-World Analogy: Diagnosing a Car Breakdown

Imagine your car starts making strange noises while driving. Your approach might be to:

- Check the dashboard for warning lights.

- Listen for where the noise is coming from.

- Consult the owner's manual or a mechanic to isolate the problem.

- If necessary, revert to a previous state (such as an earlier software version) or replace a faulty component.

Similarly, diagnosing issues in Kubernetes involves checking system "dashboard" metrics, isolating the source of the problem, and taking corrective actions.

5. Best Practices for Monitoring, Logging, and Troubleshooting

5.1. Establish a Baseline

Regularly monitor and record normal system behavior. This baseline helps you quickly identify deviations that signal issues.

5.2. Document and Automate

- **Document Processes:**
  Keep a log of common issues and the steps you took to resolve them.

- **Automate Remediation:**
  Where possible, automate responses to common alerts, such as auto-scaling or automated restarts for transient failures.

5.3. Regular Audits

Periodically review your monitoring and logging configurations to ensure they remain effective as your cluster evolves. Adjust alert thresholds and retention policies based on observed performance.

5.4. Integrate with CI/CD Pipelines

Integrate monitoring and logging into your CI/CD processes. This helps you catch issues early in the development cycle and ensures that new deployments do not introduce regressions.

5.5. Train and Practice

Regularly simulate failures and practice troubleshooting. This preparation helps you build confidence and ensures that when issues arise, you're ready to tackle them.

6. Recap and Key Takeaways

Let's summarize what we've covered in this chapter:

- **Monitoring Clusters:**
  Understanding and tracking key metrics (cluster health, resource usage, network traffic, application performance) are essential for maintaining a robust Kubernetes environment.

- **Logging:**
  Centralizing logs with tools like the ELK/EFK stack provides a detailed view of what's happening in your cluster, making post-mortem analysis and real-time troubleshooting easier.

- **Alerts:**
  Setting up alerts with Prometheus, Alertmanager, and Grafana ensures that you're immediately notified of any issues, allowing for quick response.

- **Hands-on Project:**
  We walked through deploying Prometheus and Grafana, configuring dashboards to visualize cluster metrics, and setting up alerting rules. This project serves as a real-world exercise to consolidate your monitoring and logging skills.

- **Troubleshooting Approaches:**
  Effective troubleshooting involves isolating the problem, incrementally diagnosing the issue, and employing rollbacks or redeployments if necessary. Regular practice and documentation are key to success.

- **Best Practices:**
  Establish baselines, document your processes, integrate with CI/CD, and conduct regular audits to ensure your monitoring and troubleshooting systems are always up to date.

7. Additional Exercises and Challenges

To further reinforce your learning, here are some additional exercises you can try:

Exercise 1: Create Custom Dashboards

- **Task:**
  Develop a custom Grafana dashboard that focuses on a specific aspect of your cluster, such as network latency or Pod restarts.

- **Steps:**
  Use Prometheus queries to pull in relevant metrics, arrange them in panels, and set thresholds for alerts.

- **Outcome:**
  Gain familiarity with Grafana's customization options and learn how to tailor dashboards to your needs.

Exercise 2: Simulate a Failure

- **Task:**
  Intentionally cause a failure (e.g., by overloading a Pod) and use your monitoring dashboard to diagnose the issue.

- **Steps:**
  Create a temporary load on your application using a tool like Apache Bench or a custom script, and then observe the alerts and logs.

- **Outcome:**
  Practice diagnosing issues using real-time data and improve your troubleshooting skills.

Exercise 3: Log Analysis Drill

- **Task:**
  Search for a specific error in your centralized logs using Kibana or Fluentd.

- **Steps:**
  Create a query that filters log messages by error keywords, and analyze the timeline to determine the root cause.

- **Outcome:**
  Learn how to leverage log aggregation tools to perform in-depth analysis of application errors.

Exercise 4: Alert Tuning

- **Task:**
  Modify your alert rules in Prometheus to reduce false positives and ensure that alerts are actionable.

- **Steps:**
  Adjust thresholds, add additional conditions, and test the alerts under different scenarios.

- **Outcome:**
  Develop a better understanding of balancing sensitivity and specificity in alert configurations.

---

8. Final Thoughts and Encouragement

Monitoring, logging, and troubleshooting are critical pillars in managing a healthy Kubernetes environment. By setting up robust systems to collect and analyze metrics and logs, you not only ensure the smooth operation of your applications but also gain the tools to quickly respond to issues when they arise.

Remember, every system faces challenges at some point. What sets successful teams apart is their ability to detect, diagnose, and resolve issues quickly. Your journey in mastering these skills starts with the foundational work you've done here—implementing dashboards, setting up alerts, and practicing troubleshooting. As you build and refine your systems, you'll develop a keen sense for what "normal" looks like, making it easier to spot when something is amiss.

Keep experimenting in your local cluster. Use every challenge as an opportunity to learn and grow. Document your findings, share insights with your team, and don't hesitate to reach out to the community for support. You have the tools and the knowledge to tackle any problem that comes your way.

Each time you solve an issue, you become more confident and prepared. Whether you're monitoring resource usage in a manufacturing plant or tracking application performance in a healthcare system, the strategies and tools you've learned here will serve you well. Remember, troubleshooting is as much an art as it is a science—trust your instincts, rely on your data, and keep pushing forward.

You can do this! With persistence, practice, and the willingness to learn from every experience, you will become proficient in monitoring and troubleshooting your Kubernetes clusters. Celebrate your successes, learn from your challenges, and keep refining your approach. Every metric you monitor, every alert you configure, and every issue you resolve brings you one step closer to becoming a Kubernetes expert.

Happy coding, and here's to creating robust, resilient systems that keep your applications running smoothly no matter what challenges arise!

CHAPTER 9:
ADVANCED TOPICS
AND REAL-WORLD
SCENARIOS

Welcome to the advanced chapter that takes you beyond the basics and into the exciting realm of multi-cluster management, CI/CD integration, and security best practices in Kubernetes. In this chapter, you will learn how to manage multiple clusters, build and automate your deployment pipelines, and secure containerized environments effectively. We'll also work on a hands-on project that guides you through creating a simple CI/CD pipeline that deploys to Kubernetes and cover troubleshooting tips for common pitfalls. This chapter is designed to be friendly, step-by-step, and packed with real-world examples that connect abstract concepts to everyday scenarios. So, grab your favorite beverage, settle in, and let's get started on this journey together.

1. Multi-Cluster Management

1.1. The Need for Managing Multiple Clusters

In many real-world applications, a single Kubernetes cluster isn't enough. Companies often run multiple clusters to separate environments (development, staging, production), handle geographic distribution, or manage high availability and disaster recovery. Imagine running several branches of a retail chain in different cities; each store is independent yet must operate under the same brand standards. In the Kubernetes world, multi-cluster management enables you to maintain consistency while meeting local demands.

1.2. Approaches to Multi-Cluster Management

There are various approaches to managing multiple clusters:

- **Centralized Management Tools:**
  Tools like Rancher, OpenShift, and Anthos provide a single interface to manage all your clusters. They help you standardize configurations, policies, and monitor clusters from one place.

- **Federation:**
  Kubernetes Federation enables you to manage multiple clusters as if they were a single entity. With federation, you can replicate resources across clusters and ensure that changes in one cluster are propagated to others.

- **Custom Scripts and CI/CD Pipelines:**
  For smaller setups, you might rely on custom automation that deploys configurations across clusters using your existing CI/CD tools.

1.3. Practical Considerations

When managing multiple clusters, consider the following:

- **Configuration Consistency:**
  Ensure that clusters share similar configurations so that

applications behave consistently regardless of where they run.

- **Networking and Security:**
  Each cluster might have its own networking policies, and securing inter-cluster communication is critical.

- **Resource Allocation and Scaling:**
  Distribute workloads based on regional demand or available capacity. For example, a manufacturing plant might run clusters in different locations to reduce latency.

- **Disaster Recovery:**
  Multi-cluster strategies provide built-in redundancy. If one cluster fails, others can take over to ensure continuity.

1.4. Real-World Example

Consider a global e-commerce platform that operates clusters in North America, Europe, and Asia. Each cluster handles local traffic, ensuring fast response times and compliance with regional regulations. A centralized management tool keeps track of inventory levels, orders, and system health across all clusters. In case of a regional outage, the system reroutes traffic to another cluster, maintaining seamless service for users.

2. CI/CD Integration with Kubernetes

2.1. The Importance of CI/CD

Continuous Integration (CI) and Continuous Deployment (CD) are practices that allow you to deliver code changes reliably and frequently. With CI/CD, developers can automatically build, test, and deploy their code to Kubernetes clusters. Think of CI/CD as an assembly line where each code change goes through rigorous quality checks before it reaches production.

2.2. Key Components of a CI/CD Pipeline

A typical CI/CD pipeline for Kubernetes might include:

- **Source Code Management:**
  Tools like Git host your code and track changes.

- **Build System:**
  Systems like Jenkins, GitLab CI, or CircleCI compile your code and build container images.

- **Testing:**
  Automated tests validate your code. Unit tests, integration tests, and end-to-end tests help catch errors early.

- **Container Registry:**
  Once the image is built, it is pushed to a container registry (Docker Hub, AWS ECR, etc.).

- **Deployment:**
  Kubernetes manifests or Helm charts are applied to update your cluster. Tools like Argo CD and Flux CD can automate this step.

- **Monitoring and Feedback:**
  After deployment, monitoring tools verify the health of the new release and provide feedback to the team.

2.3. Building a CI/CD Pipeline for Kubernetes

Let's break down the steps to build a basic CI/CD pipeline:

1. **Version Control and Webhooks:**
   Your repository in Git is configured to trigger pipeline jobs whenever changes are pushed.

2. **Automated Builds:**
   The CI system pulls the latest code, builds a container image, and runs tests.

3. **Image Deployment:**
   If tests pass, the new image is pushed to a container registry.

4. **Cluster Update:**
   The CD tool automatically updates the Kubernetes Deployment using the new image. Rollout strategies like blue/green or rolling updates ensure minimal downtime.

5. **Verification:**
   Monitoring systems check that the deployment is healthy. If something goes wrong, rollback mechanisms are triggered.

2.4. Real-World Analogy

Imagine a car manufacturing plant where each car goes through quality checks before it rolls off the assembly line. If a defect is found, the car is pulled from the line and fixed immediately. Similarly, a CI/CD pipeline ensures that only thoroughly tested code reaches production, and any issues are caught early in the process.

3. Security Best Practices in Containerized Environments

3.1. Securing Your Containerized Applications

Security in Kubernetes involves multiple layers, from securing the cluster itself to protecting the applications running inside containers. Following best practices is crucial to safeguard your data and infrastructure.

3.2. Key Security Considerations

- **Image Security:**
  Always use trusted images and scan them for vulnerabilities before deployment.

- **Least Privilege Principle:**
  Limit the permissions of Pods and containers. Use Role-Based Access Control (RBAC) to restrict who can perform actions in your cluster.

- **Network Policies:**
  Define policies that restrict communication between Pods. This reduces the risk of lateral movement if an attacker gains access.

- **Secret Management:**
  Use Kubernetes Secrets to store sensitive information, and consider integrating external secret management tools for added security.

- **Regular Updates and Patching:**
  Keep your Kubernetes version, container images, and host operating systems updated with the latest security patches.

- **Audit Logging:**
  Enable audit logs to track actions within the cluster. Logs provide valuable insights during security investigations.

3.3. Best Practices for Hardening Kubernetes

- **Pod Security Policies (PSP):**
  Although deprecated in newer versions in favor of alternatives like Open Policy Agent (OPA), these policies help restrict what Pods can do.

- **Network Segmentation:**
  Use separate clusters or namespaces for different environments (e.g., production vs. development) to minimize risk.

- **Monitoring and Alerting:**
  Implement real-time monitoring and alerts for suspicious activities. Integrate with SIEM (Security Information and Event Management) systems for advanced threat detection.

- **Container Runtime Security:**
  Choose secure container runtimes and configure them to reduce the attack surface.

3.4. Real-World Scenario

Consider a healthcare application managing patient records. It is imperative that sensitive data is protected at all times. By implementing RBAC, network policies, and regular vulnerability scans, the application minimizes exposure to attacks while ensuring compliance with regulatory standards. Using a CI/CD pipeline with integrated security checks (often referred to as DevSecOps) further ensures that every change is scrutinized for potential vulnerabilities before deployment.

---

4. Project: Creating a Simple CI/CD Pipeline That Deploys to Kubernetes

In this hands-on project, you'll build a basic CI/CD pipeline that automatically deploys a sample application to your Kubernetes cluster. We'll use a combination of tools to simulate a real-world scenario where code changes trigger a full deployment process.

4.1. Project Overview

In this project, you will:

- Set up a Git repository to host your sample application code.

- Configure a CI system (using a tool like Jenkins, GitLab CI, or GitHub Actions) to build and test your code.

- Build a container image and push it to a registry.

- Use a CD tool or script to update your Kubernetes Deployment automatically.

- Monitor the deployment and verify that the new version is running.

Imagine this project as setting up an assembly line for a small tech startup. Each new feature goes through a series of tests and quality checks before being rolled out to customers—all automated to ensure speed and reliability.

4.2. Step 1: Preparing Your Sample Application

For this project, we'll use a simple web application written in a language of your choice (for example, a basic Node.js or Python Flask app). Ensure your application has a Dockerfile that builds the container image.

Example: A Simple Flask Application

Create a file called app.py with the following content:

python

```python
from flask import Flask
app = Flask(__name__)

@app.route('/')
def hello():
    return "Hello, Kubernetes CI/CD!"

if __name__ == '__main__':
    app.run(host='0.0.0.0', port=5000)
```

Create a requirements.txt file:

plaintext

```
flask
And a Dockerfile:
dockerfile
```

```dockerfile
FROM python:3.9-slim
WORKDIR /app
COPY . /app
RUN pip install --no-cache-dir -r requirements.txt
EXPOSE 5000
CMD ["python", "app.py"]
```

4.3. Step 2: Setting Up Version Control

Initialize a Git repository in your project directory and push the code to a platform like GitHub or GitLab.

bash

```
git init
git add .
git commit -m "Initial commit for CI/CD demo"
git remote add origin <your-repository-url>
git push -u origin master
```

4.4. Step 3: Configuring the CI System

Depending on your chosen CI tool, create a configuration file to define the pipeline.

Example: GitHub Actions Workflow

Create a file called .github/workflows/ci-cd.yml:

yaml

```
name: CI/CD Pipeline

on:
  push:
    branches: [ master ]

jobs:
  build:
    runs-on: ubuntu-latest
    steps:
    - name: Checkout Code
      uses: actions/checkout@v2

    - name: Set up Python
      uses: actions/setup-python@v2
      with:
        python-version: '3.9'
```

```yaml
    - name: Install Dependencies
      run: |
        pip install -r requirements.txt

    - name: Run Tests
      run: |
        echo "No tests defined"  # Replace with your test commands

    - name: Build Docker Image
      run: |
        docker build -t your-dockerhub-username/flask-app:latest .

    - name: Log in to Docker Hub
      run: echo "${{ secrets.DOCKER_HUB_PASSWORD }}" | docker login --username ${{ secrets.DOCKER_HUB_USERNAME }} --password-stdin

    - name: Push Docker Image
      run: |
        docker push your-dockerhub-username/flask-app:latest

  deploy:
    runs-on: ubuntu-latest
    needs: build
    steps:
    - name: Deploy to Kubernetes
      uses: appleboy/ssh-action@master
      with:
        host: ${{ secrets.KUBE_HOST }}
        username: ${{ secrets.KUBE_USER }}
        key: ${{ secrets.KUBE_KEY }}
        script: |
          kubectl set image deployment/flask-deployment flask=your-dockerhub-username/flask-app:latest
```

In this workflow:

- The pipeline triggers on every push to the master branch.

- The code is built and tested.

- A Docker image is built and pushed to Docker Hub.

- An SSH action is used to connect to your Kubernetes environment and update the Deployment image.

4.5. Step 4: Configuring the Kubernetes Deployment

Create a Kubernetes Deployment for your application.

Create a file called flask-deployment.yaml:

yaml

```
apiVersion: apps/v1
kind: Deployment
metadata:
  name: flask-deployment
  labels:
    app: flask-app
spec:
  replicas: 2
  selector:
    matchLabels:
      app: flask-app
  template:
    metadata:
      labels:
        app: flask-app
    spec:
      containers:
      - name: flask
        image: your-dockerhub-username/flask-app:latest
        ports:
        - containerPort: 5000
```
Deploy the Deployment:
bash

```
kubectl apply -f flask-deployment.yaml
```

4.6. Step 5: Testing and Verification

Once your CI/CD pipeline is set up:

- Push a code change to trigger the pipeline.

- Verify that the new image is built and pushed.

- Check your Kubernetes cluster to ensure the Deployment is updated:

bash

kubectl get pods -l app=flask-app
- Access the application to confirm the new version is running.

4.7. Troubleshooting Deployment Issues

If your deployment fails, consider these troubleshooting tips:

- **Review CI Logs:**
  Check the logs in your CI system to identify where the pipeline failed.

- **Examine Kubernetes Events:**
  Use kubectl describe deployment flask-deployment to look for error events.

- **Rollback if Necessary:**
  Use kubectl rollout undo deployment/flask-deployment to revert to a previous stable version.

- **Verify Configuration:**
  Double-check environment variables, secrets, and network settings in your Deployment.

5. Addressing Common Pitfalls and Troubleshooting Deployment Issues

Even with robust pipelines and monitoring, deployments can encounter problems. Here are some common pitfalls and strategies to address them:

5.1. Pitfall: Image Pull Errors

- **Issue:**
  Sometimes Kubernetes is unable to pull the container image due to authentication issues or misconfigured image names.

- **Solution:**
  Ensure that your container registry credentials are correctly configured in your cluster (using ImagePullSecrets) and that the image name and tag are accurate.

5.2. Pitfall: Resource Constraints

- **Issue:**
  Pods may fail to schedule if there are insufficient resources (CPU, memory) on the nodes.

- **Solution:**
  Monitor resource usage and adjust resource requests and limits accordingly. Consider using the Horizontal Pod Autoscaler (HPA) to dynamically adjust replicas based on load.

5.3. Pitfall: Misconfigured Environment Variables

- **Issue:**
  Incorrect environment variables can cause application failures.

- **Solution:**
  Use ConfigMaps and Secrets to manage configuration data, and verify that the values are correctly injected into your Pods.

5.4. Pitfall: Network Policies Blocking Traffic

- **Issue:**
  Overly strict network policies may block necessary communication between services.

- **Solution:**
  Review and adjust network policies to ensure they allow traffic between essential components while still providing security.

5.5. Pitfall: Rollout Failures

- **Issue:**
  During a rolling update, some Pods might fail to become ready, causing a stalled deployment.

- **Solution:**
  Use readiness and liveness probes to ensure Pods are healthy before proceeding with the update. If issues occur, roll back to the previous version and investigate the cause.

5.6. Real-World Scenario: Handling a Failed Deployment

Imagine a scenario in a logistics company where a new version of an application that tracks shipments is rolled out. Shortly after the update, shipment data fails to load. By reviewing the CI/CD logs, you notice that the new image had a typo in an environment variable. The operations team quickly triggers a rollback, and the previous version is restored. This minimizes disruption and allows developers to fix the error before attempting another update.

---

6. Best Practices for Advanced Topics

As you work with multi-cluster management, CI/CD pipelines, and secure deployments, keep these best practices in mind:

6.1. Documentation and Version Control

- **Keep Detailed Records:**
  Maintain clear documentation for your configurations, pipelines, and deployment processes. Version control all your YAML files and CI/CD scripts.

6.2. Automation and Testing

- **Automate Everything:**
  Use CI/CD to automate builds, tests, and deployments. This reduces human error and speeds up the release process.

- **Test Thoroughly:**
  Implement comprehensive testing at every stage, including unit, integration, and end-to-end tests.

6.3. Security First

- **Implement RBAC:**
  Ensure that only authorized users can make changes to your clusters and deployments.

- **Scan for Vulnerabilities:**
  Use automated tools to scan your container images and code for security vulnerabilities.

6.4. Monitoring and Observability

- **Set Up Dashboards:**
  Monitor your deployments in real time with tools like Prometheus and Grafana.

- **Create Alerts:**
  Configure alerts to notify you of any anomalies in resource usage or application behavior

6.5. Continuous Learning

- **Stay Updated:**
  The Kubernetes ecosystem evolves rapidly. Keep learning from documentation, blogs, and community forums.

- **Share Knowledge:**
  Collaborate with your team and share lessons learned from both successes and failures.

7. Recap and Key Takeaways

Let's summarize the main points from this chapter:

- **Multi-Cluster Management:**

    - Understand why you might need multiple clusters for different environments or geographic regions.

    - Explore centralized management tools and federation as strategies to simplify operations.

- **CI/CD Integration with Kubernetes:**

    - CI/CD pipelines automate the process from code commit to deployment.

    - Build pipelines that include code testing, image building, and automated deployments.

- **Security Best Practices:**

    - Secure your images, implement RBAC, use network policies, and manage secrets carefully.

    - Ensure that your deployment processes include security checks and vulnerability scans.

- **Hands-on Project – CI/CD Pipeline:**

    - Build a pipeline that integrates with your Git repository, builds a container image, and deploys to Kubernetes.

    - Verify the deployment by monitoring updates and testing the application.

- **Troubleshooting and Common Pitfalls:**

- Identify issues like image pull errors, resource constraints, and misconfigured environment variables.

- Use tools like kubectl, monitoring dashboards, and log aggregators to diagnose and fix problems.

- **Best Practices:**

  - Document your processes, automate builds and deployments, continuously test and monitor your systems, and keep learning.

---

8. Additional Exercises and Challenges

To further solidify your understanding, here are some exercises you can try on your own:

Exercise 1: Multi-Cluster Deployment Simulation

- **Task:**
  Simulate a scenario where you deploy the same application across two clusters.

- **Steps:**
  Use a management tool or custom scripts to deploy your application to two different clusters. Ensure configurations and secrets are synchronized.

- **Outcome:**
  Learn how to handle multi-cluster deployments and verify that your application behaves consistently across environments.

Exercise 2: Enhance Your CI/CD Pipeline

- **Task:**
  Add a stage to your CI/CD pipeline for automated testing.

- **Steps:**
  Integrate unit tests or integration tests into your GitHub Actions (or other CI tool) workflow. Modify your pipeline so that a deployment only occurs if all tests pass.

- **Outcome:**
  Understand the importance of testing in preventing faulty deployments and build confidence in your pipeline.

Exercise 3: Implement Advanced Security Checks

- **Task:**
  Integrate a vulnerability scanning tool into your pipeline.

- **Steps:**
  Use tools like Clair or Trivy to scan your container images during the build phase. Configure the pipeline to fail if vulnerabilities are detected.

- **Outcome:**
  Learn how to add an extra layer of security to your CI/CD process and ensure that only secure images are deployed.

Exercise 4: Simulate a Rollout Failure

- **Task:**
  Intentionally introduce a misconfiguration into your deployment, then trigger a rollback.

- **Steps:**
  Modify an environment variable or image tag to cause an

application error. Monitor the pipeline, then use kubectl rollout undo to revert to a known good state.

- **Outcome:**
Gain hands-on experience with diagnosing rollout failures and practicing rollback procedures.

---

9. Final Thoughts and Encouragement

Advanced topics in Kubernetes, such as multi-cluster management, CI/CD integration, and security best practices, are vital skills for anyone working with containerized applications at scale. These techniques not only improve the reliability and efficiency of your deployments but also empower you to manage complex environments with confidence.

It's normal to feel challenged as you tackle these advanced subjects. Remember that every expert once stood where you are now—learning step by step, experimenting with new ideas, and troubleshooting issues along the way. The hands-on project in this chapter is designed to give you practical experience and help build your confidence in automating deployments and managing security.

Keep pushing your boundaries by experimenting with different tools, integrating new security measures, and refining your CI/CD processes. The lessons you learn here are directly applicable across industries—from manufacturing and healthcare to logistics and beyond. With every build, test, and deployment, you're honing skills that will set you apart as a proficient Kubernetes professional.

Stay curious, document your processes, and never hesitate to ask questions or seek help from the community. Every deployment challenge is an opportunity to learn, and every problem solved adds to your growing expertise.

You have the tools and the mindset to tackle even the most complex environments. Celebrate your progress, and remember that each step you take brings you closer to mastering Kubernetes in real-world scenarios.

Happy coding, and here's to creating robust, secure, and efficient pipelines that propel your projects forward—one commit, one build, and one deployment at a time!

CHAPTER 10: FUTURE TRENDS AND BEST PRACTICES

Welcome to the final chapter of this Kubernetes guide. In this chapter, we explore what lies ahead in container orchestration and share practical best practices that can help you stay on top of evolving technology. We will examine emerging trends that are reshaping how applications are built and managed, highlight how industries like healthcare, logistics, and manufacturing are making use of Kubernetes, and offer advice for continuous learning and improvement. We'll conclude with final thoughts and actionable next steps to help you build on the skills you've gained.

Imagine standing at the edge of a bustling city that never sleeps—a city where new buildings, innovative transportation systems, and cutting-edge technology emerge every day. In many ways, the world of container orchestration is similar, with fresh ideas and practices constantly transforming the landscape. Whether you are a developer, operations specialist, or a business leader, understanding these trends and best practices can help you prepare for what's ahead.

In this chapter, you'll find detailed discussions, real-world examples, and a hands-on mini-project that will help you experiment with emerging features. So, let's explore the future of container orchestration and discover how you can continue to grow your skills in this dynamic field.

1. Emerging Trends in Container Orchestration

The way applications are built and managed is undergoing a transformation, thanks to the rapid pace of innovation in container orchestration. Here are some key trends shaping the future:

1.1. Multi-Cloud and Hybrid Deployments

Increasingly, organizations are moving away from relying on a single cloud provider. Multi-cloud and hybrid environments allow companies to distribute workloads across different platforms, minimizing the risk of vendor lock-in and maximizing flexibility.

Imagine a farmer who grows a variety of crops across different fields to hedge against unpredictable weather. In the same way, businesses distribute their applications to ensure high availability and resilience. Kubernetes now supports multi-cloud architectures through federated clusters and centralized management tools. This means you can manage workloads running on different clouds from a single control point.

1.2. Edge Computing and IoT Integration

Edge computing is becoming more prominent as the demand for real-time data processing grows. Instead of sending all data back to a centralized data center, edge computing processes data closer to the source—reducing latency and improving performance.

Think of it like a neighborhood bakery that bakes fresh bread on-site rather than shipping it from a central factory. With Kubernetes, you can deploy lightweight clusters at the network's edge, which is particularly useful in scenarios like smart cities, autonomous vehicles, or industrial IoT where split-second decisions matter.

1.3. Serverless Architectures and Function-as-a-Service (FaaS)

Serverless computing is an approach where developers focus solely on writing code, while the underlying infrastructure automatically scales and manages execution. Although not new, the combination of Kubernetes with serverless frameworks, such as Knative, is opening up exciting possibilities.

Imagine ordering a cup of coffee without worrying about how the barista gets it ready; you simply enjoy the final product. Similarly, with serverless models, you write your function and let the system handle the scaling, provisioning, and execution. This approach reduces operational overhead and can optimize resource usage.

1.4. Artificial Intelligence and Machine Learning Integration

AI and ML are now being applied across various industries to enhance decision-making and automate processes. In Kubernetes, AI is used not only to improve application performance but also to predict resource requirements and optimize scaling decisions.

Consider a smart thermostat that learns your schedule and adjusts the temperature accordingly. Kubernetes can integrate predictive analytics to anticipate when workloads will spike and allocate resources ahead of time, ensuring smooth performance even during peak times.

1.5. Observability and Automation Advances

As clusters grow in complexity, the need for better observability becomes paramount. Advances in monitoring, logging, and tracing are enabling more granular visibility into how applications perform.

Automation tools are also maturing, allowing for more sophisticated self-healing and remediation processes.

Imagine having an assistant that not only alerts you when something goes wrong but also fixes it automatically. This vision is becoming a reality as Kubernetes environments leverage AI-powered observability and automated recovery strategies, which can reduce downtime and manual intervention.

---

2. Industry Applications of Kubernetes

Kubernetes is not just a buzzword; it's already changing the way industries operate. Here, we take a look at how sectors such as healthcare, logistics, and manufacturing are using Kubernetes to drive innovation.

2.1. Healthcare

In healthcare, the safe and secure handling of patient data is crucial. Hospitals and healthcare providers are adopting Kubernetes to streamline application deployment, ensure compliance with data regulations, and improve patient care.

- **Real-Time Data Processing:**
  Imagine a system that monitors patient vital signs in real time and alerts medical staff immediately if something unusual is detected. Kubernetes makes it possible to run such applications reliably at scale.

- **Data Security and Compliance:**
  By leveraging Kubernetes features like Secrets and RBAC, healthcare providers can enforce strict security measures.

This is akin to a hospital using secure storage for sensitive records, ensuring that only authorized personnel have access.

- **Telemedicine:**
  With the rise of telemedicine, scalable applications are needed to support virtual consultations and remote patient monitoring. Kubernetes helps deploy these applications in a way that can handle sudden spikes in user demand during health crises.

2.2. Logistics

The logistics industry relies heavily on timely and accurate data to manage shipments, track inventory, and optimize delivery routes. Kubernetes can support these requirements by providing scalable, resilient applications.

- **Fleet Management:**
  Think of a logistics company that tracks its delivery trucks in real time, adjusting routes based on traffic and weather conditions. Kubernetes can power these systems by dynamically scaling and ensuring that the data flows smoothly between different components.

- **Supply Chain Optimization:**
  In a modern supply chain, multiple systems must communicate efficiently to minimize delays and costs. Kubernetes helps integrate these systems by standardizing the deployment and management of microservices, much like a well-coordinated orchestra where every instrument plays in harmony.

- **Scalability During Peak Periods:**
  During holiday seasons, logistics companies face enormous

spikes in demand. With Kubernetes, applications can automatically scale to handle increased load, ensuring that operations continue without interruption.

2.3. Manufacturing

Manufacturing processes are becoming more automated and data-driven. Kubernetes plays a key role in enabling smart factories by managing applications that control machinery, monitor production lines, and analyze performance metrics.

- **Real-Time Monitoring:**
  Imagine a factory floor where sensors continuously feed data about machine performance and production quality. Kubernetes can host applications that process this data in real time, helping to detect issues before they become major problems.

- **Predictive Maintenance:**
  By integrating machine learning with Kubernetes, manufacturers can predict when equipment is likely to fail and schedule maintenance proactively. This is similar to a car mechanic who can foresee when a vehicle needs service based on patterns observed over time.

- **Flexible Production Lines:**
  In modern manufacturing, production lines must be adaptable to changing product demands. Kubernetes supports microservices architectures that allow production systems to be reconfigured quickly and efficiently, much like rearranging a workshop to build different products.

3. Advice for Continuous Learning and Improvement

The world of container orchestration and Kubernetes is constantly evolving. Staying current with the latest trends and best practices is essential for long-term success. Here are some tips to keep your skills sharp:

3.1. Engage with the Community

Join forums, attend webinars, and participate in local meetups or online groups. Whether it's Kubernetes Slack channels, Reddit threads, or user groups, engaging with peers is an excellent way to learn from real-world experiences and share your own challenges and successes.

- **Online Communities:**
  Participate in GitHub discussions, join Kubernetes-focused groups on LinkedIn, or follow influential Kubernetes bloggers.

- **Conferences and Meetups:**
  Attend events like KubeCon or local tech meetups. They provide insights into the latest trends and offer networking opportunities.

- **Open-Source Contributions:**
  Contributing to open-source projects can accelerate your learning. Even small contributions help you understand how large systems are built and maintained.

3.2. Experiment with New Tools and Technologies

Don't be afraid to try out emerging tools that can complement your Kubernetes environment. Experimenting in a test environment can expose you to new capabilities and ideas that may become mainstream in the near future.

- **Labs and Sandboxes:**
  Use cloud providers' free tiers or local setups with Minikube to experiment with new features.

- **Side Projects:**
  Work on personal projects that challenge you to integrate multiple technologies. A side project is an excellent way to apply what you've learned in a low-risk environment.

- **Stay Updated:**
  Follow blogs, newsletters, and podcasts related to Kubernetes and container orchestration. Keeping an eye on industry news helps you spot trends early.

3.3. Build a Personal Learning Roadmap

Set goals for what you want to learn and how you plan to achieve them. A roadmap can help you navigate the vast landscape of container orchestration and ensure that you continually build on your existing knowledge.

- **Certifications:**
  Consider pursuing certifications like the Certified Kubernetes Administrator (CKA) or Certified Kubernetes Application Developer (CKAD) to validate your skills.

- **Learning Platforms:**
  Use platforms like Coursera, Udemy, or Pluralsight to take

structured courses. Many courses offer hands-on labs that reinforce learning through practice.

- **Mentorship:**
  Find a mentor or become one yourself. Mentorship is a two-way street that can greatly accelerate your learning and give you practical insights.

3.4. Document Your Journey

Keep track of your experiments, successes, and challenges in a blog or a journal. This practice not only reinforces your learning but also provides a valuable resource that you can refer back to in the future.

- **Write Blog Posts:**
  Share your experiences on platforms like Medium or Dev.to. Explaining concepts to others is one of the best ways to deepen your understanding.

- **Maintain a Wiki:**
  Create internal documentation for your projects and experiments. A well-maintained wiki can be a lifesaver when troubleshooting complex systems.

---

4. Hands-on Project: Exploring Future Trends with a Demo Environment

To bring together the ideas of future trends and best practices, let's build a demo environment that showcases some emerging features and integrates continuous learning practices. In this project, you'll set up a Kubernetes cluster that simulates an advanced environment with multi-cloud capabilities, integrates a CI/CD pipeline, and demonstrates automated scaling based on real-time metrics.

4.1. Project Overview

In this demo, you will:

- Deploy a sample application that can scale dynamically.

- Set up a CI/CD pipeline to automate deployments.

- Integrate a multi-cloud simulation by configuring two namespaces that mimic different cloud regions.

- Implement a dashboard that shows key metrics and alerts.

- Document your process and share your findings.

Imagine setting up a futuristic control center where you can monitor multiple regions, deploy updates with the click of a button, and see real-time performance metrics. This project will not only give you hands-on experience with advanced Kubernetes features but also serve as a blueprint for managing complex, multi-region environments.

4.2. Step 1: Setting Up a Multi-Namespace Cluster

Namespaces help you divide your cluster into virtual clusters. In this project, you will create two namespaces that simulate separate cloud regions.

1. **Create Namespaces:**

bash

```
kubectl create namespace region-a
kubectl create namespace region-b
```

These namespaces act as isolated environments that can have their own resources, policies, and configurations.

2. **Verify Namespaces:**

bash

kubectl get namespaces
Ensure that both region-a and region-b appear in the list.

4.3. Step 2: Deploying a Scalable Application

Next, deploy a simple application (for example, a web server) in both namespaces.

1. **Create a Deployment YAML File for Region A:** Create a file named web-deployment-region-a.yaml:

yaml

```
apiVersion: apps/v1
kind: Deployment
metadata:
  name: web-deployment
  namespace: region-a
  labels:
    app: demo-web
spec:
  replicas: 2
  selector:
    matchLabels:
      app: demo-web
  template:
    metadata:
      labels:
        app: demo-web
    spec:
      containers:
      - name: web-container
        image: nginx:alpine
```

```
ports:
- containerPort: 80
```

2. **Deploy to Region A:**

bash

```
kubectl apply -f web-deployment-region-a.yaml
```

3. **Create a Similar Deployment for Region B:** Duplicate the file, change the namespace to region-b, and deploy it.

4. **Verify the Deployments:**

bash

```
kubectl get pods -n region-a
kubectl get pods -n region-b
```

4.4. Step 3: Setting Up a CI/CD Pipeline

Follow the CI/CD instructions from the previous chapter to set up a pipeline that updates both namespaces. Configure your pipeline to deploy changes automatically to both region-a and region-b. Use a tool such as GitHub Actions, GitLab CI, or Jenkins. Ensure your pipeline:

- Pulls the latest code.

- Builds and tests the container image.

- Pushes the image to your container registry.

- Updates the Deployment in both namespaces with the new image.

4.5. Step 4: Integrating Automated Scaling

Implement autoscaling on your application to simulate dynamic load. Create a Horizontal Pod Autoscaler (HPA) for your deployments.

1. **Create an HPA for Region A:**

bash

```
kubectl autoscale deployment web-deployment -n region-a --cpu-percent=50 --min=2 --max=10
```

2. **Repeat for Region B:**

bash

```
kubectl autoscale deployment web-deployment -n region-b --cpu-percent=50 --min=2 --max=10
```

3. **Monitor Scaling:** Use monitoring tools like Prometheus and Grafana (as set up in previous projects) to visualize how the autoscaler adjusts the number of Pods based on CPU usage.

4.6. Step 5: Creating a Dashboard

Set up a Grafana dashboard to display metrics from both regions. Customize panels to show:

- CPU and memory usage for each namespace.

- Number of replicas over time.

- Alerts triggered by autoscaling events.

Document the steps and queries you use in Grafana. This dashboard will serve as your central view into the performance and health of your demo environment.

4.7. Step 6: Documenting and Sharing Your Findings

After setting up the demo environment, create documentation that covers:

- The purpose and design of your multi-namespace simulation.

- How your CI/CD pipeline integrates with the Kubernetes cluster.

- Observations from the autoscaling and monitoring dashboards.

- Lessons learned, challenges encountered, and potential improvements.

Share your documentation with your team or publish it on your blog. This practice not only reinforces your own learning but also contributes to the broader community.

---

5. Final Thoughts and Next Steps

5.1. Embracing the Future

The world of container orchestration is moving fast, and Kubernetes is at the forefront of this evolution. The trends we've discussed—from multi-cloud strategies to edge computing and serverless integration—are already shaping the future of application deployment and management. Staying ahead means being adaptable, continuously learning, and experimenting with new tools and techniques.

5.2. Implementing Best Practices

Remember the importance of:

- **Security:** Always apply security best practices to protect your applications.

- **Automation:** Leverage CI/CD pipelines to streamline your deployment process.

- **Observability:** Invest in robust monitoring and logging to keep your systems running smoothly.

- **Documentation:** Keep detailed records of your configurations, experiments, and lessons learned.

5.3. Continuous Learning and Improvement

Your journey does not end here. The skills and knowledge you have built form a strong foundation, but the learning process is ongoing. Explore advanced certifications, contribute to open-source projects, and participate in community events. By staying engaged, you will not only refine your expertise but also be prepared to tackle emerging challenges.

5.4. Actionable Next Steps

1. **Experiment Regularly:**
   Set aside time each week to try out new features in your local or cloud-based Kubernetes environments.

2. **Join Communities:**
   Engage with fellow professionals through online forums, Slack channels, and local meetups. Sharing experiences and asking questions will accelerate your growth.

3. **Expand Your Projects:**
   Build additional projects that challenge you to integrate multiple aspects of Kubernetes—security, scalability, and multi-cluster management. Each project is an opportunity to apply what you've learned in new ways.

4. **Stay Updated:**
   Follow Kubernetes blogs, podcasts, and newsletters. Technology moves fast, and being informed will help you spot trends and adopt best practices early.

5. **Share Your Knowledge:**
   Whether through blogging, speaking at events, or mentoring others, sharing your experiences not only reinforces your learning but also helps others on their journey.

5.5. A Vision for the Future

Picture yourself as an innovator in a high-tech control room, managing a fleet of applications across multiple clouds, edge devices, and data centers. You have the confidence and tools to scale systems effortlessly, automate deployments, and secure sensitive data—all while adapting to new challenges as they emerge. That vision is within reach, and the skills you've gained in this guide are the stepping stones to making it a reality.

6. Recap and Conclusion

Let's review what we've covered in this chapter:

- **Emerging Trends:**
  We explored how multi-cloud deployments, edge computing, serverless architectures, AI integration, and

advanced automation are transforming container orchestration.

- **Industry Applications:**
  We saw real-world examples of how healthcare, logistics, and manufacturing are leveraging Kubernetes to enhance efficiency, improve performance, and ensure resilience.

- **Continuous Learning:**
  Tips for staying current, engaging with communities, experimenting with new tools, and documenting your journey were shared to encourage lifelong learning.

- **Hands-on Project:**
  We built a demo environment that simulates multi-region deployments, integrated a CI/CD pipeline, implemented autoscaling, and set up a monitoring dashboard. This project served as a practical exercise in applying advanced techniques and best practices.

- **Final Thoughts:**
  The chapter wrapped up with actionable next steps, encouraging you to embrace change, continuously improve, and share your newfound expertise.

The future of Kubernetes and container orchestration is full of possibilities. As you move forward, remember that every new challenge is an opportunity to learn, adapt, and innovate. The strategies and best practices you've explored in this chapter will help you design systems that are not only robust and scalable but also flexible enough to evolve with the changing technological landscape.

You now have a roadmap for both today's challenges and tomorrow's opportunities. Use this guide as a reference, a checklist, and a source of inspiration as you build and manage your applications. Every experiment, every deployment, and every troubleshooting session brings you closer to mastering the art of modern application orchestration.

7. Additional Exercises for Future Exploration

To ensure that you continue growing your skills, here are a few exercises and challenges to tackle after you finish this chapter:

Exercise 1: Advanced Multi-Cluster Simulation

- **Task:**
  Set up an environment that simulates three clusters in different geographic regions.

- **Steps:**
  Use namespaces or actual separate clusters, deploy a shared application, and implement a routing strategy to direct traffic based on location.

- **Outcome:**
  Learn how to manage inter-cluster communication and ensure high availability across regions.

Exercise 2: Enhance Your CI/CD Pipeline with Canary Releases

- **Task:**
  Modify your existing CI/CD pipeline to implement canary deployments.

- **Steps:**
  Configure a small percentage of traffic to use the new version while the majority continues with the stable version.

Monitor performance and gradually roll out the update if tests pass.

- **Outcome:**
  Gain experience with safe, gradual rollouts that minimize risk during updates.

Exercise 3: Integrate Security Scanning into Your Pipeline

- **Task:**
  Add a stage in your CI/CD workflow to automatically scan container images for vulnerabilities.

- **Steps:**
  Use tools like Trivy or Clair, and configure your pipeline to fail if high-severity vulnerabilities are found.

- **Outcome:**
  Improve your deployment security and gain confidence that your applications are secure before they go live.

Exercise 4: Develop a Custom Monitoring Dashboard

- **Task:**
  Create a Grafana dashboard that aggregates metrics from different clusters or namespaces.

- **Steps:**
  Write custom queries to display data such as latency, error rates, and scaling events. Include visual alerts for any anomalies.

- **Outcome:**
  Strengthen your observability skills and develop a tool that helps you proactively manage your environment.

8. Final Words of Encouragement

As you reach the end of this guide, remember that you have embarked on an exciting journey. The landscape of container orchestration is vast and ever-changing. While you may feel overwhelmed at times, each step you take builds your expertise and confidence.

Keep experimenting with new tools, share your experiences with peers, and never be afraid to explore uncharted territory. The lessons learned here—from multi-cluster management to CI/CD integration and security best practices—are valuable not just for today, but as a foundation for future innovations.

Take a moment to reflect on how far you've come, and then set your sights on the next challenge. Whether you're looking to deploy mission-critical applications in healthcare, optimize supply chains in logistics, or revolutionize manufacturing processes, the skills you've acquired will empower you to make a real impact.

You can do this. Every deployment, every automation script, and every troubleshooting session is a victory on your path to mastery. Embrace the future with enthusiasm, keep learning, and remember that you have the potential to shape how technology serves businesses and communities.

Happy coding, and here's to a future filled with innovation, resilience, and endless learning opportunities!

9 798280 501041